Tales from North Yorkshire

Leonard Markham

With Illustrations by Don Osmond

COUNTRYSIDE BOOKS
NEWBURY, BERKSHIRE

COUNTRYSIDE BOOKS
3 CATHERINE ROAD
NEWBURY, BERKSHIRE

ISBN 1 85306 256 1

Produced through MRM Associates Ltd., Reading
Typeset by Paragon Typesetters, Queensferry
Printed in England

'Ther is neea sike thing ez luck,
What cums ti yan, 'ez ti be fetched.
Good luck's t'best gitten wiv a wet vest.'
                    Old Yorkshire proverb.

Contents

YORKSHIRE – The map overleaf is by John Speede, and shows the county as it was in the early seventeenth century.

The Prophetess of Knaresborough

The world famous sorceress and soothsayer Old Mother Shipton was born in a Knaresborough cave in 1488. Her pedigree was far from noble. Her mother Agatha was an unmarried maid who hastily retired to a convent and her father was apparently Old Nick himself. Christened Ursula Southill, the strange little baby was taken in by a foster mother, the unfortunate lady soon realising the folly of her ways. Aspiring to the spell making prowess of her mother, young Ursula became a problem child, performing strange feats of illusion and mystery. And by the time of her marriage at the age of 24 to Tobias Shipton, a builder from York, she had developed a fearsome reputation.

White frocks and posies impart even the faintest comeliness to the ugliest of brides' faces, but what did Tobias, at the moment of plighting his troth, make of his bride. If beauty is in the eye of the beholder, what blindness was his if this description is to be believed.

'She was very morose and big boned, her head very long, with great, goggling, sharp and fiery eyes, her nose of an incredible and unproportional length, having in it many crooks and turnings, adorned with many strange pimples of diverse colours . . . which, like vapours of brimstone gas gave such lustre in the dead time of night.'

And there's more . . . 'She had in addition a chin of the nutcracker order, yellow skin shrivelled and wrinkled, one solitary big tooth standing out of her mouth like a tusk, neck so distorted that her right shoulder supported her head, legs crooked with feet and toes turned towards her left side, so that when she walked to the right it seemed as if she were travelling to the left.'

The new Mrs Shipton was not a home-loving type. She spurned the duties of the kitchen in favour of rhymed prophecy. The first recorded reference to her powers of prediction is contained in a pamphlet published in 1641. The pamphlet suggests that in 1530 she plied her dubious trade in York, an important religious centre being made ready for the visit of Cardinal Wolsey. His holiness was annoyed to learn that, according to Mother Shipton, he would never reach the city alive. Scorning the prediction with a threat to burn the prophetess as a witch, the cardinal set out for Yorkshire but he was arrested at Cawood and indicted for treason. He died soon afterwards. The pamphlet also refers to the devastation of London, the great diarist Samuel Pepys making a similar reference when quoting the words of Prince Rupert on the day of the great conflagration, 'Now Shipton's prophecy is out'.

Presumably, like modern day fortune-tellers, Mother Shipton earned her living by charging clients a fee. Her former consulting cave is intimidating even now, so what was it like in the gloom of the 16th century? An old poem gives us a clue:

'Near to the famous dropping well
She first drew breath, as records tell,
And had good beer and ale to sell
As ever tongue was tipped on.
Her dropping well itself is seen;
Quaint goblins hobble round their queen,
And little fairies tread the green,
Call'd forth by Mother Shipton.'

Her most celebrated predictions, all widely quoted in modern tourist brochures and leaflets, are undoubtedly hoaxes. The ascribed forecasts about the building and subsequent destruction of the Crystal Palace, the outbreak of the Crimean War and the development of ironclad ships were the work of a Brighton bookseller, Charles Hindley, who confessed his forgery in 1873. So is the whole Mother Shipton story eyewash? 'No,' say Knaresborough shopkeepers. 'Yes,' say historians, offering as evidence the silence of John Leland, Henry VIII's official antiquary who, after visiting Knaresborough in 1538, only a few years after the king ordered Wolsey's arrest, made no comment about the town's infamous lady.

But those who have felt the chill of the famous dropping well can be forgiven for believing there is some truth in the legend.

Knaresborough visitors arriving by train would be advised to take heed of one prophesy yet to come true. The picturesque viaduct over the river Nidd was originally built in 1848. As a result of poor workmanship and cheap materials, the structure collapsed and was rebuilt in 1851. Will it tumble again? Watch out, remembering the oft quoted prophecy . . . 'Mother Shipton allus said 'at t' big brig across t'Nidd 'ould tummle doon twice and stand for ivver when built a third time'!

The
Amazing Racing Pig

It is a well known fact that pigs cannot fly, but by Jupiter they can run! The famous eccentric Jimmy Hurst from Rawcliffe proved that pigs can be trained as pointers and they were used with equally good effect as fox-hunting aids in Coxwold in the early years of the 1800s. But by far the most amazing demonstration of the pig's running talents was left to a Malton farmer. He taught one particularly fleet-footed beast to race, in Derby style.

Influenced by the success of Coxwold fanciers, the farmer began his own experiments with a sty of prize pigs. He soon discovered that they were intelligent, had noses to match anything canine, were readily taught and, surprisingly, had an electric turn of speed, albeit over short distances. Buoyed by his success, the farmer spoke of the prowess of his animals in a Malton inn, boasting that his pigs could match any horse! Now Malton at that time was a nationally renowned centre for breeding race horses, the home of such outstanding celebrities of the turf as *Isinglass,* and the notion that a cloven footed beast could beat a thoroughbred was ridiculed with a mixture of disbelief, scorn and hysterical jollity. Eventually the tumult died down and the company realised that the farmer was serious. An indignant racehorse owner stepped forward to put him to the test. Honour was at stake. A mere breeder of cart horses and swine had uttered a blasphemy and he would be made to pay for his flippancy with a wager. A race was arranged with the purse to be £100. The specified two-furlong course was on level ground. The farmer was to be allowed to stable his contender in a sty at the starting point for one month to facilitate familiarisation with the ground and to allow adequate time for training. It was also agreed that whoever rode the horse would do so in the owner's colours. For his part, the racehorse owner was permitted to select the pig, to satisfy himself that fleetness was not restricted to one exceptional animal. The pact was made and the company departed to place their bets, naturally on the horse!

A suitable pig was chosen for the race and he was dubbed *Eclipse* and transferred to his temporary sty. The training then began in earnest. During the first 2 days of his ordeal, the pig was starved of food and persistently lashed by a man in a livery of orange and green. The third day dawned brighter with the offering of a bowl of swill but the blows still rained down even as the food was being poured. Ravenous, the poor pig braced himself and dipped his snout in the trough. Miraculously the beating ceased.

Continued every day for the next two weeks, the brutal ritual taught the pig that the tormentor spared the rod only when his victim was dining. 'Snouts down snuffling!' was the maxim of the day to avoid a good hiding.

So far so good. The first day of the third week arrived and the pattern of training was changed. This time the swill bucket was only shown tantalisingly to the pig for a few seconds before being carried for 50 yards up the course and left in full view of the salivating animal. With the whip cracking on his back the pig cleared the ground in record time. And over the next 6 days he learnt to run progressively faster to swill buckets placed ever nearer to the finishing line. By the end of the week he was a very fit pig.

The fourth week arrived and the pig realized that worse was yet to come. He had been removed from his chums, starved, beaten, made to run like a demented rabbit and now the ultimate horror – his arch-enemy, the whip-wielding torturer, who in the past he had always managed to outpace, had been given a horse! By the end of the final week he was even fitter still.

The day of the race arrived and the pig was rigged in a lightweight harness to prevent him bolting and was led to the start to join a saddled horse. Piggy cogitations on yet another change of routine were abruptly ended by the appearance of a jockey dressed in orange and green. As the restraints were cut, the frantic pig simply shot from the start and beat the horse by several lengths to the delight of its owner and the consternation of the bookies!

Man
The Lifeboat!

'A lifeboat it drives on with a mercy which does not quail in the presence of death, it drives on as a proof, a symbol, a testimony that man is created in the image of God and that valour and virtue have not perished in the British race.'

These words of Winston Churchill underline the respect of our island people for the lifeboatman, amongst whose ranks resounds the name of an exceptional Yorkshireman – Henry Freeman.

The son of an itinerant brickmaker, Henry was born on the 29th April 1835. After some years in Bridlington, the family moved to Flamborough where the ill-educated Henry developed an interest in the sea. In 1851 he began to work as a labourer on Lighthouse Farm, the spray-lashed acres affording him a grandstand view of a daring rescue that had a profound effect on his future career.

Trained as a brickmaker, Henry went on to take up his father's trade, first in Bridlington and then in Whitby. His employer's premature death from tuberculosis left him in sole charge of the business but the claustrophobia of the kilns spurred him to don his sea-boots. For a while, he endured life as a lowly bilge-hand, tramping the east coast waters in a variety of small craft. Soon tiring of the monotony of shipboard life, he returned to Whitby and by 1861 he was a fisherman, a long-liner occupied in the perilous pursuit of cod, haddock, ling, halibut and turbot.

Norse legend has it that the god Odin reserves one

supreme moment for the assay of mettle. Henry Freeman's warrior's test came on the 9th February 1861. It was a day for cowering. It was a day for prayer. All along the east coast, ships floundered in a terrific gale. By nightfall, 210 vessels would be smashed to pieces.

Dawn saw Henry Freeman among a party of fishermen walking in the direction of Sandsend. In the surf they spied the *John and Ann*, a Sunderland brig, driven ashore by a raging wind. Quickly commandeering a coble (a flat-bottomed rowing boat) they rescued the endangered crew within minutes. But the heroics had just begun.

The schooner *Gamma*, bulging with an unstable cargo of coal, was the next victim. Pinned on a sandbank only 400 yards from the pier she was pounded by heavy seas and her crew was in mortal danger. This time the official lifeboat was launched. As a reward for his earlier assistance, Henry Freeman, with no previous crewing experience, was allowed in the boat. Again, all hands were saved.

After slugs of fortifying grog, the men rescued the crews of the *Clara, Roe* and *Utility* in quick succession, and still the storm continued to wreak havoc. From the spyglass, two more ships were seen to be in distress. It was early afternoon, and a multitude of spectators watched as the *Flora* and the *Merchant* were blown relentlessly towards the pier. At a great speed of knots, the *Flora* crashed into the harbour and all her crew were saved. As for the *Merchant*, she ran aground only yards from safety. The lifeboat was launched. 'Now pull away,' cried the coxswain!

Dodging the matchwood from previous wrecks, with mountainous waves threatening to overwhelm his puny boat, the coxswain shouted orders to the oarsmen. Deluged in sea water, hardly able to see or breathe through the curtain of spray, they pulled and pulled again towards the frightened sailors hanging like limpets from the rigging. Driven back by cross seas, they tried once more, but in a convulsion of waves, described by seafarers as 'a knot of the sea', the lifeboat was spewed skywards, the next wave hitting it broadside and turning it turtle. Let Henry Freeman take up the story:

'When the boat turned over I was underneath her with the Gun'ale across my chest. My body was under the boat and I was looking upwards through the water. A sea struck the boat and released me and I floated free. I was wearing a new kind of cork belt, which had been sent down for trial, like the ones now used. I was the only man wearing one in the boat.'

Henry Freeman, the only survivor of the lifeboat tragedy, was awarded the RNLI Silver Medal for his bravery, but strange to say, in some quarters he received a critical press. A temperance lecturer called Thomas Whitaker wrote to the *Scarborough Mercury* attributing the disaster to drunkenness! This outrageous allegation was met with not a little hostility, an angry crowd of 5,000 rioters storming through Scarborough and flogging an effigy labelled 'WHITE-E-CUR.'

Headstrong, cantankerous, quarrelsome and ambitious, Henry Freeman was not initially a popular lifeboatman and it took some years before he had a regular place in the crew. His reputation was also marred by controversy and suggestions of lying in connection with the death of a member of the opposing crew in a coble race. However, by 1877, Freeman had his hands on the tiller and in a few short years, he became one of the most outstanding coxwains in history.

His skill, courage and unflagging determination were admirably displayed in a famous rescue of 1877. On the morning of 19th January, in appalling blizzard conditions, the brig *Visiter* floundered 4 miles off Robin Hood's Bay. Battling against a hurricane strength storm, with its sails in tatters, the ship was in imminent danger of breaking up. Immediate help was needed to save the crew but weather conditions were deemed too dangerous to launch local fishing craft or the Whitby lifeboat. Ordinary men might have wrung their hands and lit candles, but Henry Freeman, the implacable Henry Freeman who would spit in the eye of Poseidon if there was a life to be saved, announced they would go overland!

The 32 ft long lifeboat was hauled by horses and the crew through deep snowdrifts for six miles, with over 200 helpers, men women and children, in the vanguard shovelling and breaking down walls to clear a bee-line path. Along the way old ladies offered hot toddies, and, tossing their bags aside, postmen spontaneously joined in the digging, as from the Robin Hood's Bay side, a second team fought the drifts with equal intensity. After 3½ hours, the lifeboat was gingerly slid down the Bay's steep hill, almost becoming wedged on the hairpin turn by the Laurel Inn. Finally, the boat was pushed into the sea and the rescue got under way.

A further hour elapsed, the frantic pulling of splintered oars getting the lifeboat no nearer the *Visiter*. Two semi-conscious crewmen were returned to shore and this time, with a complement of 18, some double-manning the oars, the lifeboat snatched the sailors to safety and delivered them to the slip where there were rapturous cheers. The Yorkshire heart swells at such a spellbinding event achieved in such atrocious weather conditions, described by a witness so: 'The morning of the rescue, mother was washing up in the kitchen. She went out at the back to look across the Bay at the *Visiter* with the dish cloth in her hand. When she went back into the kitchen, it was frozen stiff. They had to warm it very slowly and carefully to get it off without taking the skin off her hand'.

Not long after this incredible rescue, Henry Freeman was disgraced by a conviction for stealing fishing lines. Ordered to pay a £15 fine (2 years' wages) or face going to prison for 2 months, he chose the former and spent some time paying off his dues and restoring public confidence in his character. It is a tribute to his fortitude and resilience that he managed to redeem his reputation and he continued saving lives right up to his retirement at the grand old age of 63.

A 20 stone, 6 feet hulk of a man with a formidable appearance and persona – an image that would grace any mackerel tin – Henry Freeman died in 1904. For 80 years, the adopted town to which he gave so much could not even muster a headstone. Thankfully, this lamentable transgression has recently been remedied and Whitby now honours the man with a simple epitaph:

'Henry Freeman
Died 13th December 1904
Only Survivor of the Whitby Lifeboat Disaster of 1861.

Coxswain of the Whitby Lifeboat 1877-1899.

During His Service He Helped To Save Over Three Hundred Lives.'

The Penny Hedge Penance

The most bizarre penance in ecclesiastical history was decreed by a Whitby abbot in 1159. Odder still is its hell-like perpetuity. Over 800 years, on every Ascension Eve, three penitents must perform their solemn duty by erecting a token fence – the penny hedge – in the mud of the Esk. Presided over by the Hutton family, lords of the manor, the ceremony is still carried out in the traditional manner, although the hedge is now planted facing the harbour as a benefit to the photographers.

What grievous sin warranted such atonement? The foulest crime in Christendom – the murder of a priest!

The crime was perpetrated by two noblemen, Ralph de Percy, Lord of Sneaton, William de Bruce, Lord of Ugglebarnby, and Allatson, a Fylindales freeholder – who in the autumn of 1159 were enjoying boar-hunting in the forests around Eskdaleside near Sleights. Passions inflamed by the excitement of a long chase, the hunters pursued a terrified boar into the cell of a hermit engrossed in prayer. The startled priest, in attempting to protect the beast, was fatally stuck by a lance. Attended by Abbot Sedman, he died some days later in the hospital of Whitby Abbey.

This vilest of medieval crimes was normally punishable by execution and the forfeiture of estates, but at the intercession of the dying hermit, the murderers were spared, on condition that they, and their heirs, forever and a day, perform an annual act of contrition. They were charged with constructing a woven palisade of sticks on

21

the estuary shore. Cut with a penny knife, the sticks had to endure for three successive tides or the men would suffer the loss of all their possessions.

Throughout recorded history, initially with much solemnity and public humiliation, and today with a great deal of visitor and media attention, the ceremony has been duly enacted in Whitby harbour. At the appointed hour, sticks are collected in the Eskdaleside wood, the instructions prescribing nine stakes, four stowers or struts, and nine yethers, or branches for intertwining. The stakes are rammed a yard apart into the mud and when the fence is completed, in accordance with ancient custom, a ceremonial horn is blown and an expiatory shout 'Out on ye! Out on ye! Out on ye!' rings out across the water.

A peculiar and intriguing aspect of the ceremony is the stipulation that it may cease if high water ever prevents the hedge from being erected. Although the date of Ascension Eve and the times of the tides vary from year to year, within living memory the tides have always obliged.

But what priestly subterfuge led to the choice of this queerest of punishments? Some say the tradition is pure invention, suggesting that the symbolic erection of a fence derives from the ancient necessity of annually reinstating boundaries. But most Yorkshire folk prefer to side with the romantic Sir Walter Scott, who alludes to the tradition in *Marmion*:

'Then Whitby's nuns exulting told,
How to their house three barons bold
Must menial service do;
While horns blow out a note of shame,
And monks cry, "Fye upon your name!
In wrath, for loss of sylvan game,
St Hilda's priest ye slew":
This, on Ascension Day, each year,
Must Herbert, Bruce and Percy hear.'

The Legend of Semerwater

North Yorkshire has a number of enigmatic lakes and tarns, each with its own aura of magic and mystery. Malham and Gormire radiate their own particular charms, but neither has the biblical potency of Semerwater. In the sequestered country flanking the shortest river in Yorkshire, there hides a legend of truly chastening proportions.

The dales surrounding the lake of Semerwater near Bainbridge, even in comparatively modern times were a kingdom apart, a remote and rugged expanse of forests and isolated farmsteads. Superstitions nurtured by tales of druidical sacrifice and Roman occupation still cling to the area and to the infamous lake, the Carlow Stones at its foot being proclaimed as the Devil's slingshot. In a contest with another demon, Beelzebub is said to have hurled the stones together. And there is proof . . . 'One has t'ould lad's fingerprints on it!'

The legend of Semerwater dates from pre-Christian days, from a time when Roman legions, having dislodged the persistent Brigantes, established a camp on nearby Addlebrough. In the valley below, a prosperous town developed, proclaiming its wealth in a procession of minarets and golden cupolas. This latter day Sodom, with all the opulence and debauchery of the Old Testament town, was visited by an angel. Disguised as an old man, dressed in the poorest clothes, the pale and emaciated spirit toured the streets begging for food. He found only scorn and rejection and was evicted from the town's precincts.

Outside the walls of the town, a decrepit old couple had built a rude hovel, and it was to this humble abode that the angel then came. Seeing the wretchedness of the vagrant, the old man ushered him to the fireside and bade him share a frugal meal of bread and cheese. Overwhelmed at the kindness and generosity of his hosts, the angel bestowed a solemn blessing and retired to rest his head. Rising next morning he thanked the old couple for their hospitality but his smiles turned to tears as he faced the accursed town, uttering the malediction:

'Semerwater rise, Semerwater sink,
And swallow all the town
But this little house
Where they gave me meat and drink.'

With a fanfare of fire and brimstone the golden town was swamped and all its inhabitants apart from the old couple were lost beneath the flood.

Some say that the legend is based on a much embroidered tale about a landslide afflicting an ancient village settlement in the valley floor. Other observers insist that the story of the avenging angel is the gospel truth, claiming that at certain times of the year, apparitions and spectral images of the ruined spires can be seen through the pellucid waters of the lake; an unfathomable mystery.

And this is not the only such conundrum in this wild and wondrous land. Atop the crowning peak of Addlebrough, a giant once stood resting on a journey from Skipton Castle to Pendragon. Tired from his exertions, he dropped to the ground and like the town below he was swallowed up, the earth magically closing over him and his load. His load? A chock-full chest of pure gold. And it has never been found!

George Hudson Railway King

Every age produces its incendiaries, outstanding men and women who grab Fate by the throat and shoot for the stars. Having achieved success, some lose it, their abilities stained by corruption, extravagance and greed. A classic example of the rags to bare breeches story is that of George Hudson, railway entrepreneur, Lord Mayor of York and swindler extraordinaire.

Born in 1800, George Hudson, the son of a Howsham farmer, left home to escape the shotgun advances of a potential father-in-law. Apprenticed to York linen drapers Bell and Nicholson, he quickly rose through the ranks, marrying a daughter of one of the partners and becoming a partner himself in 1823.

In 1827, Lady Luck smiled benignly on young George. He inherited the astonishing sum of £30,000 from a great uncle, the fortune provoking ambitions of grandeur and sparking off avaricious passions soon to be directed at a number of highly speculative but potentially extremely profitable schemes.

In double quick time, the haughty and newly dandified Hudson bought a grand mansion in Monkgate, York, and he became a firebrand member of the Tory party, acting as the treasurer and 'briber-in-chief' of an organisation riddled with corruption.

By 1833, Hudson had become a leading local politician and a shrewd businessman. In that pivotal year he attended a meeting to discuss the concept of linking York

to the expanding national rail network. Appointed as treasurer to a committee charged with investigating the options, he recruited a competent engineer and spent several weeks in detailed study of proposals for a route between York and Leeds. Although the plans were abandoned, Hudson gained valuable experience for the pioneering years ahead.

A fateful meeting in the summer of the following year with the famous engineer George Stephenson, set Hudson on a course that was to change the geography of the north. A partnership between the two men was struck to build hundreds of miles of railways. Hudson pledged to raise capital and to organise company bureaucracy to deliver the schemes, and Stephenson was charged with the monumental task of construction. At Hudson's insistence, York was to be the network's heart.

Plans were drawn up, investment capital was secured and the project began amid great optimism. At the same time, Hudson advanced his political career, becoming Lord Mayor of York in 1837 after one of the most corrupt campaigns for decades. Surrounded by sycophantic toadies, the newly invested mayor wasted public funds in a disgraceful exhibition of ostentation and self aggrandisement, prompting one commentator to record 'The new Lord Mayor seemed to see in his term of office a grand opportunity to feast his way into the hearts of his fellow citizens and . . . drown all discord and opposition in champagne and sherry.' A year of indulgence and merry-making at the council's expense, was crowned in 1838 by celebrations to mark the coronation of Queen Victoria. Grocery vouchers for 14,000 of the 'lower orders' of citizens were provided free, the poor were regaled with an 'excellent and substantial breakfast' and Hudson and his cronies dined at the Guildhall. The events concluded with an imperial procession conducted on a scale unprecedented in York and perhaps without rival in any provincial town. At the head of the 1½ mile cavalcade

27

of civic, military and trade dignitaries was the robed and bespangled Hudson, leading the line of sparkling stagecoaches.

With Hudson as its chairman, the newly created York and North Midland Company opened the line to York in 1840. Connecting with the North Midland Railway, it created a direct link with London. For the first time ever, York travellers willing to change at Normanton, Derby and Rugby could be in the capital in time for tea!

Passengers and shareholders in the new company, which paid a handsome dividend, were ecstatic, although even at this early stage in Hudson's ascendancy, there were rumours of mismanagement and false financial accounting.

By 1844, Hudson, dubbed 'His Steam Majesty', presided over 1,000 miles of track and he controlled eleven seemingly immensely profitable railway companies. The whole nation became gripped by railway mania, even the poorest in society clamouring to invest their hard earned funds in new lines. In 1845, 800 consortia competed for parliamentary permission to build new lines and for a time it seemed that the frenzied speculation and huge investments involved would siphon off funds, undermining other national industries.

Ignoring the persistent calls for restraint by some members of the establishment, Hudson, denigrated by Carlyle as a 'big swollen gambler' continued apace, developing new routes and promoting his other interests. A local hero, he became the chairman of the York Union Bank, part-proprietor of several influential newspapers and, to massage his bloated ego, he acquired lavish estates, notably Londesborough Hall in the East Riding and Newby Park near Thirsk.

A ruthless and powerful millionaire controlling an empire of profitable routes, Hudson used his mayoralty to oppose proposals for the construction of the monopoly-breaking Great Northern line from York to London.

Almost without dissension, the council voted to heed their master's voice, one sole newspaper sounding a note of rebuke. 'There is no knowing but Mr Hudson may some day take it into his head to seize the Minster and convert it into a station . . . there are few, if any, would cry "nay".'

Comeuppance year was 1848. Hudson had invested over £30 million in an abortive venture to develop an east coast line. In the ensuing investigation by commissioners and investigative committees, years of deceit and deception were finally revealed. His shady business practices were made public and an avalanche of share offloading and public outrage caused his bankruptcy and expulsion from the council. In London, his Madame Tussaud's waxwork was melted down, the magazine *Punch* joining in the celebrations:

> 'Toll for the knave!
> The Royal GEORGE is gone,
> His last account is cook'd
> His work of doing done.'

In debt, Hudson retired to Newby Hall. Civic ignominy followed. The council removed his name from the roll of aldermen and Hudson Street was renamed Railway Street. Dependent on an annuity from friends, he lived in disgrace for the rest of his life, succumbing to the combined effects of gout and angina in 1871.

A victim of his own greed, George Hudson will long be remembered for his unlawful ways. And yet, true to his vision, York is a major hub of the railway network and perhaps it has secured from his legacy the biggest prize of all, for with Hudsonian fierceness, it boasts the best railway museum in the land.

All
for Love

Most men plight their troth in gold. As a token of love, the ring symbolises permanency and endurance, and yet even this fickle band cannot compare with the constancy of the Beggar's Bridge. Built in 1619 by Tom Ferris as a monument to his sweetheart, it has spanned the Esk at Glaisdale for nearly 400 years.

Born in Lastingham in 1568, the bright-eyed son of a sheep farmer, Tom Ferris was apprenticed at the age of 14 to a Hull ship owner. During holiday periods Tom returned home and he spent some time with relatives in the village of Egton, where, according to tradition, he met Agnes Richardson, the comely daughter of the rich and influential squire of Glaisdale.

The couple immediately fell in love, meeting whenever possible to caress and weave their dreams. Squire Richardson, however, frowned on Tom's lowly status, and although he did not forbid the relationship outright, he did all in his power to end the affair.

In addition to parental objections, Tom also had to contend with a geographical obstruction. In the 16th century, the river Esk was prone to flooding and the amorous suitor had, on occasions, to wade neck deep to reach the trysting place. He would frequently arrive dripping and bedraggled at the squire's front door, his appearance further reducing his chances of wooing his potential father-in-law, for marriage was his aim.

The couple resolved in secret to tie the knot and Tom Ferris boldly confronted the squire to seek his permission. 'The affrontery of the upstart! A clod marrying my sweet Agnes? Never!' was the reaction, but Tom was uncowed. 'Sir,' he continued resolutely, passion flaming in his chest, 'If I, by my own endeavour, secure a fortune to match your own, will you relent?' The squire smiled knowingly. 'But will Agnes wait that long?', he asked. 'She will!' boomed Tom. 'Then you have my permission to marry. Return with your crock of gold, but until then I forbid you to speak to Agnes. Now leave!'

Downhearted at the rejection and incensed at being denied even a parting kiss, Tom prepared to leave. His apprenticeship concluded, he was signed up to Queen Elizabeth's navy and was Whitby bound, to join a fleet being made ready to fight the Armada. But first he went to take a clandestine farewell of his lady.

A midnight candle flickered in Agnes's window, the lovers' semaphore signalling that the squire was abed. Tom wanted to rush to his girl and tell her of his plans, explaining how he proposed to plunder the Spanish Main and to return laden with treasure. But this May night in 1588 was particularly wet and his usual fording place was submerged in a torrent of water. In vain did he look for an alternative crossing, realising that it was too risky to try to jump across. Reluctantly he turned away, looking back at intervals at the candle still burning, and left to join his ship without even a parting kiss.

The brave Tom Ferris fought and won, so impressing Sir Francis Drake that he invited him to join further expeditions against the Spanish fleet. With the Queen's blessing the sea-dogs swept all before them, and in 1592, Tom Ferris, the 24 year old veteran buccaneer, returned to London, having helped capture a galleon. It was laden with gold.

Dressed in the finest clothes and riding a magnificent stallion, Tom returned to Glaisdale to claim his prize.

Steadfastly, Agnes had waited, never giving up hope of being his bride. Tom took her in his arms, kissed her sweetly on the lips and pulled out a magnificent ring. The squire said nought but smiled.

Tom and Agnes were quickly married in the local church, afterwards settling in Hull, where Tom became a successful businessman. In 1618 Agnes died, after many years of happy marriage. But Tom never forgot her. In 1619, in memory of that fateful night over 30 years before, he erected the Beggar's Bridge, impressing his initials in the stone parapet. The little bridge has survived floods and tempests to this day.

The Secret Garden

A dd a palm tree, and there is a beach in Yorkshire to compete with any in the Caribbean. Add an alpenhorn and there is a view in this blessed county to vie with anything in Zermatt. And this secret paradise is to be found just to the south of Masham. Unsullied and crisp packet-free, it enjoys a degree of anonymity, its sylvan splendours hardly disturbed by so much as a boot.

Hackfall, near the village of Grewelthorpe, is an arboreal garden situated in a natural amphitheatre high above the river Ure. First planted and set out with eccentric follies in the 18th century and once described as 'one of the most complete bird's eye landscapes in the world', Hackfall has, in recent decades, reverted to wilderness, and yet paradoxically this only adds to its romantic appeal.

The garden was conceived by William Aislabie as a contrast to his more formal works at nearby Fountains Abbey. Influenced by an Alpine journey undertaken as part of a grand tour of Italy in 1720, and financed by profits accrued from investments in the South Sea Bubble, Aislabie had a grand plan to create a stupendous landscape taking Nature as his canvas. As a site for his designs, he chose a gorge rising 300 feet above a bend in the Ure and he began planting specimen trees and constructing a web of interlinking pathways leading to grottos and dells.

The centrepiece of the scheme was the Forty Foot Fall, a picturesque cascade fed by a discreetly hidden reservoir. Around this feature were a number of other jewels, the Fountain Pond and notably the Alum Springs whose upper cascade of tinkling sweet water flowed from a source half hidden by luxuriant mosses and harts' tongues. And there were a number of heroically inspired buildings, the octagonal Fisher's Hall named in honour of the head gardener, The Rustic Temple and at the highest point, offering giddy views of York Minster and Roseberry Topping, Mowbray Point. Once completed, the garden was widely applauded. Turner came here to paint, Wordsworth recommended a stop-over en route to the Lake District and with the advent of rail travel, tourists came in droves.

A century after Aislabie's pioneering works, a Grewelthorpe nailmaker named James Casmey published a poem, *A Voice From Hackfall* advertising a gala opening of extended facilities by Lord Ripon in May 1859. New pathways had been laid out, a tearoom had been provided and transport was arranged from Ripon Station. Despite the small entrance fee, Hackfall became a major tourist haunt, being particularly attractive to young romantics.

With the decline in tourist interest, Hackfall was sold to a Ripon timber merchant around 1930. All saleable timber over 10 years old was felled and the estate was subsequently bought as a private retreat, public interest waning with the passing years. With the threat of commercial exploitation in 1987 came a sudden realisation of the local and national importance of Hackfall, and the Hackfall Trust was set up with the objective of securing the garden and restoring it to its former glories. The Woodland Trust has recently entered the fray, acquiring a 999 year lease on the estate and promising to work in partnership with the Landmark Trust who have shown an interest in conserving Aislabie's buildings. Today prospects are good for Hackfall to regain its former popularity when once again visitors will be able to marvel at its hidden treasures.

'To Hackfall's calm retreats, where nature reigns,
In rural pride, transported fancy flies,
O! bear me Goddess to these sylvan places,
Where all around unlaboured beauties rise.'

Harrogate's First Lady of Mystery

In 1926, the spa town of Harrogate was the scene of a most singular mystery that not even Hercule Poirot could fathom.

It was in that year that the creator of literature's most punctilious detective was involved in a strange affair that beguiled the nation. Where was the respectable 36 year old plumpish red-head who mysteriously went missing on the night of December 3rd leaving her car dangling over the edge of a precipice? A bushfire of speculation made front page news and every police force in the country was put on alert to find Agatha Christie.

The facts surrounding her disappearance are as fascinating as any fiction. Before she vanished, Agatha, so the official story goes, spent a miserable evening in her Sunningdale home contemplating her crumbling marriage, agonising over the romantic liaison between her husband, Colonel Archie Christie and his mistress Nancy Neele. The couple were at that moment sharing an illicit evening as house party guests in Godalming. As Agatha grieved, an overwhelming compulsion to escape spurred her to action.

Tossing a few belongings into her Morris Cowley convertible, she abruptly left her home and drove off into the night. Then her car broke down. She managed to start

it with the help of a passing farm labourer and drove on, almost ending the final chapter of a scintillating career at the bottom of a 120 feet chalk pit, at Newlands Corner in Surrey.

A local constable inspected the scene, put two and two together and came up with multiple theories. There was no body, so the conclusion was attempted suicide, murder or kidnapping. The scene of the crime gave few clues, Agatha's driving licence, attache case and oddments of clothing doing little to lift the fog.

Meanwhile in Harrogate's Hydro Hotel (subsequently renamed the Old Swan), a rather charming young lady nonchalantly signed the register as Mrs Neele and retired to powder her nose. Fashionably dressed, she came down to dinner and ate well. Afterwards, she mingled, conversed wittily with other visitors, danced the Charleston to the strains of Harry Codd's Hydro Dance Band, accompanied herself on the piano and gave a rendition of *Softly Awakes My Heart* at the lounge concert.

After a refreshing sleep and a hearty breakfast, she scanned the morning newpapers, and, animated by media speculation about the missing author, eagerly discussed the headlines with her fellow guests, wryly commenting on how the police description of the lady neatly matched her own!

Despite the wide publicity and the publication of a wanted poster in the *Daily Mail* offering £100 reward for information about the whereabouts of the runaway, 'Mrs Neele' managed to maintain the deception. But then two eagle-eyed musicians in the band, Bob Tappin the drummer and Bob Leeming the saxophonist, began to wonder. They conferred. They examined the photograph. They surreptitiously studied the object of their curiosity. And they argued with their wives about contacting the police, deciding at the end of the discussions that they would do nothing. A wifely ultimatum ended the debate, 'Ring the coppers or I will!'

Next evening, unbeknown to 'Mrs Neele' who had departed to change for dinner, the police arrived accompanied by Agatha Christie's husband, Colonel Archie Christie, newly arrived from Sunningdale. Around 7.00 o'clock, lusciously dressed in pink georgette, his wife tripped casually down the stairs. And they bagged her! Her reaction was to express delight at the arrival of brother Archie!

Amnesia following a car accident was the generally accepted verdict, and certainly her autobiography insisted this was the case. But was it? Other conclusions could be drawn from the evidence.

Without question the Christie's marriage was on the rocks and the colonel's affair was common knowledge. Any woman would feel aggrieved at being deceived and a clever woman with talents for weaving labyrinthine tales that keep the reader guessing to the last page, would perhaps arrange a suitably confusing retort. It could be argued that the precariously positioned vehicle was designed to restrict the police search to the immediate area, while she went north, leaving her husband to run around in the cold supervising the dragging of local lakes, the national press hot with suppositions and theories and sales of her books rocketing, while she shook a leg with Harry Coddswallop!

Whatever the real truth of the Harrogate affair, Agatha left her husband and after her divorce she married the archaeologist Sir Max Mallowan and lived happily ever after, leaving an unsolved mystery that will run and run.

Where Was The Navy?

The First World War was but 4 weeks old. Protected by the waters of the North Sea and the might of the most powerful navy in the world, Kaiser Wilhelm's principal adversary felt safe – until, out of the early morning fog on Wednesday, December 16th, 1914, appeared the pride of the German navy. The peaceful Yorkshire towns of Whitby and Scarborough were in for a shock. Sailing from the Wilhelmshaven base, under the overall command of Admiral Franz von Hipper, a powerful battle group consisting of 9 cruisers (the capital ships included *Seydlitz, Moltke, Von der Tann, Derfflinger* and *Blücher*) and several destroyers deployed unseen, prepared for simultaneous attacks on Hartlepool and Scarborough.

The bombardment of Scarborough commenced at 8.05 am, two cruisers blasting around 500 high explosive shells into the resort. Opening up from the South Bay in a 20 minute unopposed barrage, the German gunners hit numerous targets including the Grand Hotel – the billet of the Yorkshire Hussars – the Royal Hotel, the lighthouse, St Mary's parish church, the Town Hall in Gladstone Road and a number of private homes and boarding houses in Stepney Avenue and Wykeham Street. Directing their fire for several minutes at a supposed military installation, the Germans targeted a range of red-brick barracks near the castle. Thankfully, the barracks, although destroyed, were empty.

With their typical northern phlegm, the residents of Scarborough quietly pursued their daily occupations throughout the bombardment. In this baptism of fire, there were numerous reports of stoicism.

Milkmen and postmen continued their rounds oblivious to the dangers. Letters in hand, one poor soul, Alfred Beal, paid for his disdain with his life, dying only 20 yards from the letter box of Dunollie on Filey Road. Although early communion at St Martin's church was disrupted by three shells, the Archdeacon continued with the service, announcing that the congregation were as safe there as anywhere else. An old lady whose home had been damaged by shell fire remarked 'Yes, it's a pity, but I wouldn't have minded so much if I hadn't been doing my bit of cleaning.' Another stalwart, when asked to retire to the cellar for safety replied, 'I'll no go doonstairs, if the Lord wants me to be kilt, He'll see to it any road.' Yet another lady, on being told that the German navy was pounding the town scoffed, 'Hey! Is it only guns? I was frightened it was thunder'.

The patients of the hospital also behaved bravely. Casualties whose injuries were less serious than those who needed urgent surgery showed great patience and the greatest willingness to help, and several inmates in great pain quitted their beds, making way for those with more dire needs. The most poignant and uplifting remark of the day was uttered by a little girl who rushed up to the door of her house crying out joyfully, 'It's all right now, mother, here's father.'

The mood was captured by a special correspondent of *The Times* who wrote, 'The shells which shattered the buildings of Scarborough have made no impression on the spirits of the people. Nothing could be more praiseworthy than the manner in which the town passed through its ordeal and has returned to its normal life. The people of Yorkshire are proverbially hard to impress . . . Even the Admiralty announcement that such incidents will not affect naval policy has evoked practically no criticism. Scarborough accepts its risks.'

As the smoke cleared and the cruisers steamed north

for a final assault on Whitby, the full impact of the shelling was revealed. The damage was terrible and 19 civilians, whose numbers included young children, lay dead. Another 80 were injured. Although Scarborough bore her ordeal well, for years afterwards there was great puzzlement and consternation in the town at the apparent shortcomings of our defences. 'Where was the Navy?' asked the coroner before the dreadful task of interment began. The answer, a secret not to be disclosed until well after hostilities ceased, would have made the mourners howl.

Unbeknown to the German Commander-in-Chief, Admiral Friedrich von Ingenohl, the German coding system had been breached, and his intention to launch a so called tip-and-run raid on the English coast was in fact anticipated. The British Grand Fleet had been mobilised and from the fastness of Scapa Flow, the 3rd battle Squadron of eight pre-dreadnought battleships was ordered to steam south. However, Admiralty hopes of intercepting the German task force were dashed because of poor communications and confused intelligence.

Although details of the missed opportunities were not made public, regrets and recriminations within the naval service were rife. Lieutenant Filson Young of HMS *Lion*, one of the ships in the shadowing force, summed up the frustrations of the Admiralty. 'The accounts of the horrible casualties to women and children in the bombarded towns were particularly affecting; the shelling of defenceless towns was something new in naval warfare, and the Admiral's mortification at having been narrowly thwarted in inflicting punishment on the raiders was intense.'

On the other side of the water Kaiser Wilhelm presented Admiral Hipper (known in Blighty after the attack on Scarborough as the 'child killer') and his vainglorious crews with medals, and they were spurred on to further domination of the high seas. However, all was to end ingloriously in the scuttling of their fleet in the wastes of Scapa Flow after the end of the First World War.

Scorton's
Silver Arrow

Northern Yorkshire is indubitably the archery capital of
the world. Men of this shire were in the vanguard
of the fray at Agincourt, that well known bowman Robin
Hood loosed his shafts throughout the county and old
England's finest archery tournament is held annually in
the village of Scorton near Richmond.

Ancient records suggest that the contest had its unlikely
origins in the bedroom antics of a local beau, whose
shenanigans with an amorous serving maid led to parental
outrage and banishment. The disgruntled lover made off
with a family heirloom, an ornamental silver arrow, which
was subsequently either given or sold to a Mr Henry
Calverley. A sporting gentleman who had a passion for
the butts, Calverley decided to put his acquisition to good
use, and on the 14th May 1673, in the company of 20
like-minded friends, he founded the Society of Archers,
donating the silver arrow for annual competition. With
breaks only during the war years, the Ancient Scorton
Silver Arrow Tournament has been a colourful county
fixture ever since.

First laid down by the illustrious band of 21, the
unaltered competition rules stipulate two-way shooting at
separate targets at 100 yards range. Using both traditional
longbows and modern high-tech weapons made from
composite materials and laminates, archers attempt to
pierce the 3 inch inner golds with two shots allowed at
each chosen target. The coveted silver arrow and the

society captainship for the ensuing year are awarded for the first bullseye, other dead-eye Dicks receiving minor prizes – a silver bugle, a sword, gold and silver medals and various small sums of cash paid, with a sublime indifference to decimalisation, in old shillings.

Strict rules, great ceremonial, and the sporting by many contestants of the traditional attire of the greenwood infuse this ancient contest with a sense of fun, fermented by buttside proclivities for strong ale and spirits. Rumbustious archers toast each shot, teasing their fellow competitors and trying to provoke a curse, the archer thereby incurring fines levied for the benefit of the parish poor. The action continues throughout the day with a break for lunch, each competitor being honour bound to break bread with his rivals or (rule 25!) pay his share of the competition expenses and forfeit the privilege of shooting in the next round. At the end of the competition, the archers retire for a grand tea and the presentation of the prizes. The tankard salutes to the indiscretions of a Scorton rake last well into the night.

When the festivities are done, the merry men retire with their prizes, the worst shot of the day receiving a silver spoon inscribed on the back with the entreaty 'Withhold your laughter friends'. Not surprisingly, the spoon receives scant respect. Years ago, one beneficiary used the implement for dosing his 7 little children with bedtime gruel. Over the year the milk teeth assault wrought such damage that dad had to commission the local smith to bind the end of the spoon in silver.

The annual competition for the Scorton Silver Arrow is open to gentlemen archers of not less than 21 years of age. At the captain's discretion, foreign nationals may compete, and whilst today invitations are extended to our EC partners, the burghers of Crecy and Agincourt are not expected to be represented.

Leucippotomy

The only example of leucippotomy in Yorkshire is white, has four legs and resides in Kilburn. Whether you are atop York Minster or on Brimham Rocks in the Dales, low cloud excepting, it cannot be missed. There it is on the horizon, over there on the hillside to the left. Hurrah for the White Horse of Kilburn!

The word 'leucippotomy' was coined by a well known authority on equine hill figures, Morris Marples. Those ancient fertility symbols, more usually associated with the chalkland geology of the English Downs, are eye-catching landmarks and heritage features of the English countryside.

Compared to the aged bloodstock of the southern counties, the White Horse of Kilburn is a colt, but in true Texan style, ours is much bigger. It is 314 ft long and 228 ft high, occupying an area, on a 1 in 4 escarpment on the Hambleton Hills, of some 2 acres. It is said that 20 people could stand on the grassy pupil of its eye, although walking on the horse, because of the recurring problems of erosion and damage, is not allowed.

The horse was conceived and presumably funded by a Kilburn-born businessman, Thomas Taylor, who ran a successful provision store in London with his brother. Impressed at the beauty of the Uffington White Horse in Oxfordshire, Taylor wrote to Kilburn's schoolmaster, John Hodgson with a commission, enclosing a sketch of his ideas. A part time land surveyor, Hodgson enthused at the proposition, and prepared an outline sketch. The proposals were agreed by Taylor. Roulston Scar was selected as the most appropriate site, and with the assistance of local workmen and school children the work was completed on the 4th of November 1857. An old Kilburn resident, Thomas Goodricke, has left us a rhyming history of the event:

> 'Then thirty-one men of Kilburn
> Accustomed to the spade,
> Went to work right heartily,
> And soon the plot was bared.

It couldn't have been easy: the plot is on a slope of about 30 degrees, which is believed to be steeper than any other White Horse in the country, but Mr Goodricke lays down the difficulties:

> 'For only one man had a fall,
> And rolled right down the hill,
> But as they saw he was not hurt
> It caused a lot of mirth
> When an avalanche of sods came down,
> Which pinned him to the earth'.

Taylor was delighted at his creation, but his legacy has left something of a financial burden for the local community. The horses from southern stables are etched in chalk and are reasonably maintenance free. Our charger costs a little more to rectify the inadequacies of shifting clay and a light soil.

In the original delineation, 6 tons of lime were used. Between 1857 and 1920, however, this gradually disappeared as a result of cracking and landslip. Alarmed at the disintegration of the horse, which by now was a popular landmark, the residents of Kilburn set up a fund to tackle the problem. The original fund trustees were George Bolton, a farmer, Reverend H A Hawkins, the village vicar, and furniture maker Robert 'Mouseman'

Thompson, whose rodent trade mark has become as famous as the horse.

Using the interest generated from an investment of £100 in 5% War Loan Bonds, the horse was, for a while, regularly limed, the whitening being assisted by applications of spent carbide, a brainwave purchase by Robert Thompson. Perhaps he ought to have stuck to carving, for the rains came and washed the spent carbide away!

The interest on the War Loan Bonds dropped to a pitiful 3½% in the 1930s and the deterioration of the horse thereafter simply galloped along. So much so, that by the end of 1963 the spectre of the knacker's yard loomed large. There was deep concern in the community and elsewhere and an emergency meeting was called to plan action. Mr J Weston Adamson of Oldstead Hall was elected as chairman of a restoration committee, and a qualified civil engineer was enlisted to report on the condition of the horse. After exhaustive field trials to test the suitability of different whitening agents, an order was placed for the restoration to begin and a brochure was published asking for financial contributions to the rescue scheme. By the end of 1964 over £3000 had been collected. This was spent on restoring the horse to its original shape, the provision of a system of drainage, loose scree removal and surfacing with a bonding of cement set with chalk chippings. 'Now that has been done,' said Mr Adamson, 'for the first time in its life the horse actually has a chalk surface.'

Since the major restoration works were carried out, the horse has been constantly maintained under the direction of the Kilburn White Horse Committee. An aerial survey was carried out in 1974 and in 1976 pedestrian access was improved and incorporated in the Forestry Commission's 1½ mile White Horse Walk. As long as visitors resist the temptation to mount the beast they are encouraged to explore and to offer donations to meet the perennial vet bills as minor surgery is always required.

Seen from a multitude of vantage points in Yorkshire, including Greenhow Hill (27 miles), Brayton Barff near Selby (34 miles) and from Queensbury, west of Bradford (41 miles) the White Horse has become an arresting feature of our countryside, a beauty spot on the face of the fairest county in England, an example of leuccippotomy at its best. 'Lucy what? Why it's now't but a fancy hoss scrape!'

The
Wild Rose
of Towton

'Oh, the red and the white Rose, as all the kingdom knows,
Once were emblems of foes in a sad and bloody work;
When old England's noblest blood was poured out in a flood,
To quench the burning feud of Lancaster and York.'
Attributed to Lord Ravensworth

In a meadow at Towton grows a wild rose with white petals tinged with pink, which has come to symbolize one of the bloodiest battles ever to take place on English soil.

Dawn – 0643 hours – 29th March 1461. The momentous day breaks cold and grey, a mischievous wind fanning the camp fires of two opposing armies. The instruments of death are honed and sharpened. Thirty seven thousand men choke on their last crusts. By nightfall all will be hacked to death or will be mortally injured. The Wars of the Roses are about to reach their gory climax.

It is Palm Sunday. A funereal bell tolls from the church of All Saints in Saxton as on the ridge nearby a strategically positioned Lancastrian army of 50,000 men under the command of the Duke of Somerset prepares for battle. The Lancastrian King Henry VI is absent from the field. Esconced in York with Queen Margaret, he declines to fight on the Sabbath.

There are scores to be settled this day. In the Yorkist ranks to the south, the Earl of March, Edward Plantagenet, son of the Duke of York who was so brutally killed and decapitated only three months before at the Battle of Wakefield Green, rallies his 60,000 men. The perpetrator of the atrocity, Lord 'Bloody' Clifford, has already paid for his crime with an arrow in the throat. Riding in front of the assembled troops, augmented by a contingent of Burgundians, Edward exhorts, 'No Quarter! No prisoners!'

It is mid-morning now. Snow begins to fall. A fickle wind from the south blows full into the faces of the Lancastrians. The Earl of March orders the attack. Lord Fauconberg's archers loose a single flight of arrows and step back. Fooled into thinking that the infantry assault is about to begin, the Lancastrain bowmen shoot blindly into the darkening sky. The ruse is repeated until the Lancastrian quivers are empty. The misdirected arrows are collected and returned with deadly effect.

The Lancastrians move forward. The battle is enjoined with sword, bill and mace. In the worsening blizzard, the warriors fight to the death, 'as if the battle was the Gate of Paradise'. Corpses and the bodies of the dying lay everywhere, the red stains of war splashing the newly fallen snow. The contest is evenly matched. For a time, the Lancastrians sense victory. The Duke of Somerset, thinking the battle is won, permits his troops to plunder and strip the dead. Alarmed at the prospects of rout, the Earl of March rallies his men, giving those who have no stomach for the fight permission to quit the field. But brave souls who will honour his banner are promised a share of his fortune and those who will slay deserters are offered handsome rewards.

The slaughter continues with renewed violence and barbarity. Then from the south, come 5,000 Yorkist reinforcements. The Lancastrian left flank is repulsed and the tide of battle turns.

At 1515 hours the carnage is at its height on the pastures christened in gore, Bloody Meadow. The Lancastrians are in retreat in the north-west, tumbling down the steep banks towards the swollen waters of the Cock Beck. Struggling to discard their steel carapaces, drained by the exertions of battle and hampered by their wounds, some soldiers stumble and drown. Others are cut down in the mire, 1,000 bodies forming a bridgehead of butchered flesh. Crimson flows the Cock, its haemorrhaging flow discolouring the Wharfe and Ouse downstream. Onward press the jubilant Yorkists, pursuing the vanquished foe towards Tadcaster and York, where Henry and his queen prepare for flight to Scotland.

Noble heads, grisly souvenirs, are hacked from bodies for public display on Micklegate Bar, and the white rose standard is raised as dusk falls. The Earl of March triumphantly enters York with his macabre booty. King Henry VI has already flown for his life. The cheers ring out for King Edward IV!

Today, on the site of this great battle, the wild rose – the Towton Rose – its white petals tinged, it is said, with the blood of the fallen – still grows. The longstanding claim that this most ephemeral of flowers has been genetically altered by the copious amounts of blood that once drenched its roots, are sadly untrue. There is no scientific substance to the legend, yet, like the Flanders Poppy, the tender Towton Rose has come to represent one of warfare's bloodiest contests.

Taking the Cure

The medical world rejoiced in 1576 when William Slingsby discovered the Harrogate spa. Here was an elixir, a magic lotion, a libation, a laxative, a cure all, a linctus for life. Encouraged by the exaggerated claims of the many doctors who flocked to make their fortunes, Harrogate developed as a hydropathic Lourdes, offering virtual immortality for all who would take 'The Cure.'

Slingsby walled and paved the surroundings of his Tewit Well spring, suggesting that its waters 'did excell the tart fountaines beyond the seas as being more quicke and lively, and fuller of mineral spirits.' Before the end of the 16th century, the spa was recognised and recommended by the medical profession and rich and poor 'whose putrid rags lie scattered up and down, and it is doubted whether they do not wash their soares, and cleanse their besmeared clouts', flocked to this and other sites.

Over the next two centuries, scores of other health-giving springs were discovered, including the Sulphur or Shaking Well and the Bogs Field (Valley Gardens) and, gradually the commercial exploitation of the waters took hold. Bath tubs were installed in lodging houses and sick visitors were immersed in heated sulphur water to cure all manner of ailments. The author Tobias Smollett has left us this report of a typical treatment: 'Mr Mickle-whimmen recommended a hot bath of these waters so earnestly, that I was over-persuaded to try the experiment. He had used it often with success, and always stayed an hour in the bath, which was a tub filled with Harrowgate water, heated for the purpose. If I could hardly bear the smell of a single tumbler when cold, you may guess how my nose was regailed by the streams arising from a hot bath of the same fluid. At night I was conducted into the dark hole on the ground floor, where the tub smoked and stunk like the pot of Acheron in one corner, and in another stood a dirty bed provided with thick blankets, in which I was to sweat after coming out of the bath. My heart seemed to die within me when I entered this dismal bagnio, and found my brain assaulted by such insufferable effluvia. . . . I should certainly have run distracted, if the rarefaction of my blood, occasioned by the Stygian bath, had not burst the vessels, and produced a violent hemorrhage . . .'

Street corner boys, scruffy urchins with an eye for a fast farthing, pedalled brimful beakers, and so-called water women, the pitcher fillers and transporters, clamoured for business, resorting to pressure selling of the most awakening kind. They burst into the bedrooms of sleeping visitors in the early morning, crying out, 'I am pretty Betty let me serve you,' or 'Kate and Coz Dol, do let we tend you.' The contemporary description of these ladies is not very flattering . . . 'their faces did shine like bacon rind. And for beauty many vie with an old Bath guide's ass, the sulphur waters had so fouled their complexions.'

Over the years, more lodging houses were built and these were joined by fashionable inns and hotels, the developing social cachet attracting as many bon viveurs to the resort as invalids. And there was an influx of doctors and medical men of all descriptions, some with dubious qualifications and all offering wonder cures and relief from pain.

Examining the literature and promotional leaflets of the day one might be forgiven for thinking they were descendants of the Spanish Inquisition. Or that they had entered into secret pacts with the boarding house owners and hoteliers, whereby visitors would be tempted with the choicest viands and nectars to render the body more needful of treatment.

'For the treatment of this complaint, bathing in the warm sulphur baths of Harrogate is considered indispensable; and to soften the scales and facilitate their removal, something like soaking, for a longer period than may be necessary in many other complaints, will be desirable.'

The ailment here described by Joseph Frobisher, eminent senior surgeon to the Harrogate Baths Hospital in 1842 is leprosy! He goes on to stress the efficacy of the waters to treat baker's itch, fish-skin disease, apoplexy, chlorosis, diabetes, dropsy, gout, scrofula and the vapours. Although the majority of his recommendations are spurious in the extreme, he does leave us with one piece of advice on eating habits which we all should heed today: 'masticate, denticate, grind, munch, chew and then swallow.'

In later years, barbarism reached new heights with the introduction of technology, hideous new machines being harnessed in the endless assault of stoical flesh. There were peat baths, foam baths, effervescent baths, paraffin wax baths, douches, mud packs and, in 1905, the Harrogate System of Intestinal Lavage, for the treatment of nervous disorders, fibrositis, appendicitis and constipation.

The normal duration of 'The Cure' was three weeks. Always a progressive authority, Harrogate council provided a host of amenities for visitors to the town, even setting aside a vast acreage of land, originally intended to provide one of the largest municipal cemeteries in Europe. Thankfully, writers such as Smollett diverted attention to more carnal pursuits, and The Stray remains a beautiful green expanse for the enjoyment of visitors to the spa town of Harrogate to this day.

The
Devil's Arrows

Prominent from the A1 near Boroughbridge, the Devil's Arrows have been the source of fascination for centuries. Three giant megaliths of millstone grit, the stones are most probably part of a complex of Neolithic and Early Bronze Age monuments – including Thornborough, Cana and Hutton Moor henges – stretching for over 11 miles north. Projecting 18 feet, 21 feet and 22½ feet, the stones are buried to an average depth of 5 feet and they each weigh up to 36 tons.

So much for the sober business of weights and measures. How were the stones transported to Boroughbridge, and what were they used for? The first intriguing question may never be answered: we can only stand in awe of an otherwise primitive civilisation and marvel at their apparent knowledge of fulcrums and pulleys. As for the second conundrum, we can conjecture that the stones were a focus of druidical ceremonies and we can be certain that during the Roman occupation of these shores (the Roman settlement of Isurium Brigantum was nearby) they were employed as metae – the turning points in chariot races.

But the story of how they came to be known as the Devil's Arrows begins with the apostles. With missionary zeal, they had set out from their English base in Glastonbury to convert the northern tribes. The fiercest of the Yorkshire hordes were the Brigantes, whose principal town was Iseur, the centre of an empire ruled by fear and strange religious rights. Ritual burnings were commonplace. Men, women and children were placed in wicker cages adorned with sacred mistletoe and offered to the gods in a magical clearing of oaks.

Dressed in a wolf skin cape, the pagan king received the apostles. White robed Druids sat at his feet, incanting malevolent odes and demanding, encouraged by a stranger in their midst, that the visitors be taken to the sacrificial grove for execution. The king silenced them and invited the apostles to explain their mission. Then he rose in reply: 'Truly you have come on a strange errand: we are believers in and devout worshippers of the one supreme god, as you pretend to be. Do we not yearly offer up on his altars hundreds of human victims to propitiate his good will? What more would you have? We believe what you do, and a great deal more, for we have a host of minor deities whom we pay adoration to. Methinks you had better return to your own country and not trouble us with your visions. We are content with our own belief, which teaches us that when we die the souls of those who have done justly will pass gradually into a higher and higher sphere, until at length, when perfectly purified, they will become absorbed in the essence of the Deity, or become an inferior god; whilst those of the wicked men will be transformed to the bodies of inferior and unclean animals and will eventually be annihilated'.

After this speech, the apostles answered with divine eloquence that touched the king's heart, but he was confused at a creed that contradicted all his beliefs. He postponed discussions to another day, suggesting that the assembly reconvene at a later date on Roulston Scar in the Hambleton Hills.

Arrangements were made and the conference was attended by the king, his acolyte priests, many warriors, some of whose naked bodies sported tattoos depicting the sun and moon and mythical beasts, and the apostles.

The orations began, but after a short while, there was an interruption. A bearded stranger climbed onto a rock projecting over the debating ground and introduced himself as a high priest. 'Welcome', greeted the king.

The apostles expounded the gospel truths and the multitude were thoughtful until the stranger once again resumed his stony pulpit to vehemently declare the superiority of paganism saying . . . 'We are told that man was made perfect and was at the same time fallible: that God is immutable and yet repented: that a creature, the work of His hands, has become His rival and from what we hear has become ever more potent than his Maker; has set up a rival kingdom and is able to wrest from the hands of God three-fourths of the beings whom he creates, a god who is asserted to be omnipotent. Can these facts be compatible with reason, and can you, as men of sense believe them?'

There was loud and rapturous applause for the tirade, but in his rage, the stranger had entangled his cloak. A cloven hoof was spied, its contact with the rock causing the surface to become white hot and molten.

'Harken oh King!' warned an apostle. 'I have told you of the arch-enemy of God and mankind, who tempted the first man to sin, and still lures men to perdition: behold he – even he – is present in this assembly, and has been addressing you in advocacy of the false religion, which you, in your ignorance maintain. Him will I unmask . . . Satan! I defy thee in the name of the Saviour of mankind, I command thee to display thyself in thy proper person, and depart hence to the hell from whence thou comest'.

In an instant, the Devil was revealed in all his deformity, the hideous demon rising up in acrid clouds of sulphur and showers of sparks. Away he flew with the giant boulder clinging to his hoof. Converted by the revelation, all the Brigantes embraced Christianity and all were baptised.

The Devil meanwhile was set upon revenge. In fleeing the convention he had lost the giant boulder in mid flight, 7 or 8 miles from Roulston. Retrieving his stone, he split it into 4 hefty pieces which he hurled at Iseur with the curse:

> 'Borobrig keep out of the way,
> For auld Boro town I will ding down'.

Miraculously, the stones were intercepted and they landed harmlessly way off target. One has been lost to the centuries, but three remain to this day.

The Father
of Aerial
Navigation

It is a little known fact that the world's first aeroplane flight took place in Brompton Dale near Scarborough. The facts are hard to believe, but the well documented evidence is indisputable. The laurels go to a pioneering Yorkshire inventor. Given a suitable engine, he would have trounced the Wright Brothers by 50 years!

The genius in question was Sir George Cayley. A radical thinker with wide ranging interests, a visionary scientist in the mould of Da Vinci, Cayley was born in 1773, in an age when the possibilities of manned flight were thought as fanciful as magic carpets.

Cayley succeeded to the baronetcy in 1792 on the death of his father, inheriting the family estates at Brompton. A gregarious, highly inquisitive and inventive family man, Cayley devoted much of his energies to experimentation, devising over the years a host of engineering and mechanical marvels. He built and patented a device for caterpillar traction, declaring that 'the impediments and resistances of every sort of road, land, morass and water will be obviated' and he invented the self-righting lifeboat. Concerned about the increasing incidence of railway accidents he championed the cause of safety, recommending the use of two-way tracks and the installation of fog signals. He also pioneered schemes for drainage and flood control, suggesting that the frequent inundation of Malton could be relieved by the construction of a relief channel – his most enduring and visible achievement – the Scalby Cut which reaches the sea north of Scarborough. His agile mind also grappled with the conundrums of optics and acoustics, but he is remembered most for his work on aerodynamics. So much so that the president of the Societe Française de Navigation Aerienne suggested that his name should be 'inscribed in letters of gold on the first page of the aeroplane's history'.

Even at the age of ten, Cayley, inspired by the invention of the balloon, was evolving theories on the principles of flight. A dedicated observer of natural phenomena, he studied the mechanical properties of birds, concluding that 'a globe is by no means the best shape for obviating resistance to air'. By 1804 he had built a model glider with a cross-shaped articulated tail. Buoyed by the success of its maiden flight, he wrote: 'It was very pretty to see it sail down a steep hill, and it gave the idea that a larger instrument would be a better and safer convenience down the Alps than even the sure-footed mule'. The results of his experiments were published, and the problems of mechanical flight were, for the first time, classically defined: 'To make a given surface support a given weight by the application of power to the resistance to air'.

In 1809 Cayley launched a large 300 sq ft glider with similar successful results. He went on to design the first wheeled undercarriage, he assessed the potential of the 'whirling arm' or propeller as a means of propulsion and he elucidated the fundamentals of aeroplane construction, stressing the importance of weight control, air resistance and stability. In the monumental year of 1852, a new glider design was published. Excepting the absence of wing flaps, this design boasted all the refinements of the modern aeroplane. A prototype to test the theories in the field was constructed. But 140 years ago, test pilots were hard to come by. Enter Sir George's coachman! The inventor's granddaughter takes up the tale:

> 'Everyone went out on to the high east side and saw the start from close to. The coachman went into the machine and landed on the west side about the same level. The coachman got out and when the watchers had got across, he shouted: "Please Sir George, I wish to give notice. I was hired to drive, not fly."''

This short, tentative hop of only 140 ft across Brompton Dale is universally regarded as the first manned flight in a heavier than air craft. The achievement should have caused a sensation, but the idea of man taking to the skies floundered like the proverbial lead balloon. Cayley was convinced that his invention had a practical future, and although he admitted that 'a hundred necks will have to be broken before all sources of accident can be ascertained and guarded against' he confidentially predicted . . . 'that we shall be able to transport ourselves and families, and their goods and chattels more securely by air than water, and with a velocity of from 20 to 100 miles per hour'.

Sir George Cayley died at the ripe old age of 84 in 1857. His passing is commemorated by few monuments, although a silver disc, engraved by him to show the principles of fixed wing flight, is preserved in the Science Museum at Kensington. Despite his towering achievements, few Yorkshire folk know of his existence. And yet a mere 140 years after his death, you can almost hear the old man chuckling from the family vault in Brompton's All Saints church. Looking up to the heavens he smiles smugly, as an RAF Tornado performs a victory roll.

The Royal Prisoner
of Bolton Castle

If ever stars were crossed, they were Mary Stuart's. Born in Linlithgow Castle on December 7th 1542, she entered a violent world enflamed by jealousy and ambition. A ravishing and an impetuous beauty, Mary was married to the dauphin of France in 1558, spending her early years amidst the gaieties of the French court. On the death of Queen Mary of England, claims to the English throne were made on Mary's behalf by her grandmother, the eldest daughter of King Henry VII. But England already had a queen, Elizabeth I.

The widowed Mary returned to Scotland in 1561 and there began a series of adventures which led to her downfall. Her followers were routed at the Battle of Langside in 1568 and she was imprisoned. Escaping to England, she attempted, unsuccessfully, to secure the favour of Elizabeth, who kept her prisoner for 19 years.

With a retinue of ladies and servants, the 26 year old Mary was escorted to the grim fortress of Bolton Castle in Wensleydale in 1568. She was placed in the custody of Lord Scrope and assigned the services of Sir Francis Knollys, who taught her English. Mary was given a draughty chamber in the south-west tower and allowed the use of a spacious drawing room, with splendid views of the river Yore. An energetic woman, full of ambition and passion, she was courteously treated and on occasions her captors allowed her, under strict supervision, the temporary freedom of the hunt. On one such outing, chafing at her incarceration, Mary plotted her escape.

A resourceful woman who had taken the opportunity to reconnoitre the land, Mary decided to make a break for freedom. Evading the attention of her guards, with the help of an attendant who lowered her from her turret, she crept from the castle and went east, but the desperate queen was recaptured after covering only 4 miles. She was intercepted on Leyburn Shawl at a place known to this day as 'Queen's Gap'. Mary was returned to Bolton and Elizabeth was informed of the escape. Predictably, the guard was tightened.

Shortly after her recapture, Mary and her 40 strong entourage were ordered to leave Bolton Castle. After only 6 months in Wensleydale, the party, clutching the few remaining trappings of royalty, filed out of the courtyard heading for Tutbury Castle in Staffordshire. There, the confinement continued.

But some tantalising relics remain in Yorkshire to mark the passing of the fiery queen. In her Bolton bed-chamber a pane of glass scratched with her initials was a poignant item of curiosity for centuries. This was irreparably damaged many years ago, and now only the spirits of her lonely room remain, together with a fascinating item of correspondence. Her first letter written in English addressed to 'her good schoolmaster' Sir Francis Knollys begins: 'Mester Knoleis, I heve sum neus from Scotland . . .' The text continues craving the tutor's indulgence for the poor quality of the writing, explaining that the author had 'neuur vsed it afor'. The letter ends affectionately, 'thus affter my commendations, I prey God heuu you in his kipin. Your assured gud frind, MARIE R'. There is a delightful postcript: 'Excus my iuel writin thes furst tym'.

But the most intriguing relic of all is Mary's ghost, which is said to haunt Nappa Hall.

After one of her jaunts into the wild woods above the Yore, Mary spent two days as a guest of Sir Christopher

Metcalfe in the elegant surroundings of Nappa Hall. For a time she forgot about her troubles and enjoyed 'song, mirth and minstrelsy', leading the dance with her host. Amidst dark decades of gloom and foreboding such interludes must have been the fount of sweet memories. Is this why she haunts Nappa Hall? A visitor to the hall describes the apparition: 'I was in the hall, playing hide and seek with the farmer's little girl, a child of about four years old. The hall was dimly lighted by a fire, and by a light from a candle in a room in the east tower. While [we were] at play, someone entered the hall from the lower end, and walked towards the dais. Thinking it was the farmer's wife, I ran after her, and was going to touch her, when she turned round, and I saw her face. It was very lovely. Her dress seemed to be made of black velvet. After looking at me for a moment, she went on and disappeared through the door leading to the winding stone staircase in the angle of the turret of the west tower. Her face, figure and general appearance reminded me of portraits of Mary Queen of Scots.'

Mary's end was sad. She was accused of complicity in the Babington conspiracy, and was beheaded at Fotheringay Castle on February 8th 1587.

The
Newby Park
Ferry Disaster

Fox hunting can be fatal. And death is not just confined to the fox, as this tragic story will show.

February 4th, 1869, one of the blackest days in Yorkshire's sporting history, started out in jovial and optimistic mood. A special train had been chartered to convey hunters and spectators to a meet of the York and Ainsty Hunt at Stainley near Ripon, and over the conviviality of the stirrup cup, the talk was of ace fox hunter Sir Charles Slingsby and his famous mount Saltfish.

The hounds were whipped in, the hunting horn was blown and with whoops and whelps the crimsoned posse set off in the direction of Newby Hall. Riding hard, the hunt soon flushed out a fox. A wily veteran of the chase, the fox adopted a previously successful tactic of crossing the river. This was the beast that had on two occasions that season outwitted Sir Charles, but this time the hunt master was determined he should not escape.

With the hounds barking from the far bank, Sir Charles decided to cross the river by the Newby Park Ferry. A Heath Robinson contrivance consisting of a boat and a manually operated chain and cog-wheel, the ferry was particularly unstable in times of flood, and on that fateful day the Ure was running high.

Perspiring from a long chase, the horses were loaded

and the ferry was pushed from the bank. But the highly strung Saltfish suddenly took fright and, with its rider's wrists knotted in the reins, it jumped overboard, became entangled in the chain, and the boat simply capsized. At first, Sir Charles struck out for the boat, but seeing it upset, he decided to swim for the shore. Sadly he never made it to the bank and the outstretched hunting whips. Cramp took hold and Sir Charles drowned.

A hunter named Lloyd was under the boat fighting in a melee of thrashing legs. An Eton swimming champion, he extricated himself and set off with powerful strokes for the shore but he falterd, the weight of his heavy boots and hunting apparel dragging him down. From the bank, Captain Robert Vyner and William Ingilby saw his plight and both dived to the rescue. For several seconds they kept him afloat, urging him to cling to their shoulders. Lloyd's excessive weight threatened to drag his rescuers down and with calm dignity and powerful nobleness of spirit, he released his grip and gave up the struggle.

Of the two further fatalities, Robinson seems to have drowned almost immediately, and Orveys was found next day further downstream with a hunting whip still tightly clutched in his hand.

Saltfish, the immediate cause of the accident, was saved. As for the fox, he saved his brush and roamed unmolested for the rest of the season. Out of respect for the dead the York and Ainsty cancelled its programme until the following year.

Saint
Jacundus

A roué of the first water, a fat, jolly fellow with a propensity for fine ale and wines, Brother Jacundus was recruited to the brotherhood of monks in a way strange even by God's standards. In celebrating the installation of a new Lord Mayor in York at the close of the 15th century, he over-imbibed. Remorseful at his indulgence, in groggy repentance he joined the brotherhood of St Leonard's Priory, the sober impact of his solemn vows and lifelong commitment to The Lord only dawning when the vapours cleared.

For a whole year he stoically endured the torment of frugality, tantalised by thoughts of hot pasties and ale until, on the anniversary of his acceptance as a brother, his resolve broke.

The temptations of York Fair descended on the town, mirthful sounds permeating the cloistered realm of St Leonard's. Determined to enjoy an interlude of jollification, Brother Jacundus stole the porter's key and a sum of money from the prior's purse and escaped by the lodge gates as his fellow brothers slept.

Several hours melted away in an orgy of rollicking fun, Brother Jacundus exhausting his illicit funds on peep shows, rides and in the purchase of prodigious quantities of gingerbread and liquor. But the hour of retribution was at hand.

Despatched from the priory, two brothers tracked Jacundus to the fair and discovered the sinner, tankard

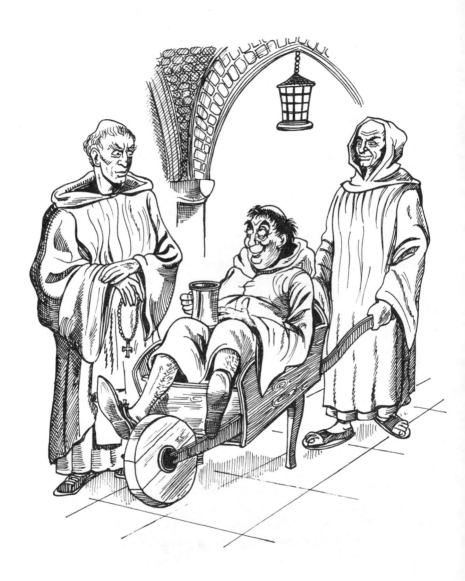

in hand, in the boat of a see-saw, lilting:

'In dulce jubilo-o-o
Up, up, up we go-o-o'.

Escape proved impossible. The quarry was apprehended
but a problem arose. Pot-bellied monks slosh-full of ale
and malmsey are not easily carried. So they fetched a
wheelbarrow.

The sinner was presented before the thunder-faced
prior, who decided to assemble the whole community of
monks for an instant trial. Hiccupping, his eyes spinning
around in their sockets, Brother Jacundus was duly
presented before the court and asked 'How do you plead?'
His reply was:

'In dulce jubilo-o-o'
Up, up, up we go-o-o'.

The court deliberated and found the defendant guilty of
gross misconduct. Sentence was passed and Brother
Jacundus was happily led away, totally oblivious to his
fate. Some hours later, he awoke and wondered at the
blackness. With only bread and water for sustenance he
found himself in a niche in the priory cellar. The entrance
had been bricked up!

A less worldly monk might have been resigned to
entombment and a slow atoning death, but however sweet
the cup, it could not, reasoned Brother Jacundus, warrant
eternal rest. He resolved to escape and began kicking and
pushing against the unseen walls. Suddenly he was
blinking in a heap of rubble and found himself in the cellar
of the adjacent abbey of St Mary's.

Dusting down his habit, Jacundus nonchalantly joined
a group of new found brothers. None spoke, for they were
Cistercians pledged to silence, and none thought to
question the visitation, assuming that the chubby

newcomer in their midst was a novitiate. Over the ensuing year Jacundus gradually integrated into the life of the abbey and supped with the abbot, praising God for his great deliverance.

After a year, on the very anniversary of his incarceration, it came to pass that the abbey victualler, the trusted monk who held the keys to the wine cellar, died and Brother Jacundus was asked to assume responsibility for the community's libations.

Brother Jacundus immeditely celebrated his promotion with a binge, toasting his luck in copious draughts of burgundy. He became hopelessly drunk and he was still singing when they walled him up! Again he was to face an agonising end with only bread and water for sustenance.

In the cloisters of his former priory next door meanwhile, there was great lamentation, for the prior had suddenly died and melancholy dirges filled the air. The cellarer was despatched to fetch wine for the final salutes. Nearing the casks, he dropped his pitcher and fell to his knees in utter terror and wide-mouthed incredulity upon hearing the strains of:

'In dulce jubilo-o-o,
Up, up, up, we go-o-o',

emanating from the very spot where twelve months previously, Brother Jacundus had been buried alive. He rose to his knees, looked to heaven in awe and tripped up the stairs to break the incredible news to the brothers.

'He's truly alive!' declared the monks in chorus, working frantically with their bare hands to demolish the tomb. 'And praise the Lord! The bread and water is as fresh as ever. It is a sign from God. It is a miracle! Come Saint Jacundus, you are to become our new prior.'

In the years to follow, Jacundus must have reflected that the ways of God are mysterious indeed.

The
Conquest of
Gaping Gill

Drip . . . drip . . . drop: a myriad drops, dissolving, cleaving, scouring, black hole-carving over aeons, creating the deepest and most awe inspiring natural shaft in Great Britain.

At a depth of 340 feet, Gaping Gill Hole, in the windswept highlands dominated by the massif of Simon Fell and Ingleborough north of Clapham, was formed by the action of water, pummelling and grinding the porous limestone rock. This most celebrated of Yorkshire potholes, riddled with over 7 miles of passages and galleries, remained until comparatively recent times, a geological embodiment of the infernal pit, a repository for human sacrifice, an object of fear and loathing and the supposed den of elves and trolls.

For centuries men conjectured that the abyss was created by gas rising from bones washed into the depths by Noah's flood, and it was not until the middle of the 19th century that scientific appraisals and tentative explorations began.

A geology professor, T McKenny Hughes, began the debate about Gaping Gill's origins, and he was the first explorer to probe the hidden depths, discovering a surface passage now know as Jib Tunnel or Lateral Passage. Using only primitive experimentation, Hughes predicted the depth of the main cavern to within a few feet, although his trials with wooden markers, cast into the depths in the hope of retrieval downstream, came to nought.

Around 1842 (although this date is open to some discussion) John Birkbeck, a pothole pioneer from Settle, attempted the first deliberate descent of the main shaft. His first problem was the Fell Beck, a mighty and incessant flow of water swilling into the pot in a plume of foam and spray and falling a distance equivalent to twice that of Niagara Falls. Birkbeck decided that the beck would have to be diverted, and at great expense he employed an army of helpers to cut a channel – the 'Birkbeck Trench' half a mile upstream. With the threatening deluge removed, Birkbeck attempted two perilous descents reaching a ledge, subsequently named in his honour, 190 feet down. The susceptibility of natural fibre ropes to chafing and the constant bombardment of dislodged stone made any deeper penetration foolhardy and Birkbeck retired content in the realisation that he was the first human being to gaze into the cathedral-like splendour of the great chamber.

In 1882, Alfred Ernest Clibborn emulated his predecessor's delvings but he got no further than the eponymous ledge. For over 100 years exploration ceased, until 1895, when an involuntary near free fall descent by Edward Calvert raised the Yorkshire pluck. Whilst traversing Ingleborough in bad weather, Calvert unknowingly crossed a snow cornice sculpted over the 30 feet wide hole and dropped down thankfully only as far as the ledge. His survival prompted plans of conquest but he was to be beaten to the history books by a Frenchman, Edouard Alfred Martel.

Already famous for his subterranean exploits on the other side of the Channel, Martel was invited as a guest speaker at the Geographical Congress in London in August 1895, and he took the opportunity to contact the owners of the Ingleborough Estate to make arrangements for a visit to Gaping Gill. His arrival in Clapham with hundreds of feet of rope ladders and perforated boots (to let the water out!) provoked excitement and much speculation and by the time of the actual attempt on the shaft, a large crowd had gathered.

Birkbeck's trench was repaired and by 1st August all was ready. Wooden stakes were driven into the peat, ladders and ropes were belayed, a telephone line was rigged up and there were final checks on lanterns, candles, magnesium flares and a flask of rum. Martel kissed goodbye to his wife, knowing that in the event of mishap there were no rescue volunteers, and he began his descent, calling out 'Let go gently'.

Despite the diversion of Fell Beck, a copious flow of water continued to percolate into the shaft, and within a few minutes of beginning his descent, Martel was soaked to the skin and was numb with cold. Then, at a depth of 130 feet, the line snagged and he was left pirouetting in space, shouting into the telephone. 'Hello! Hello!' he cried. 'What is the matter? I am in a cascade of water and certainly not warm. Hurry up. Hurry up.'

The snag freed, Martel reached the ledge and paused for breath wondering what the next few yards would bring. He pressed on deeper into blackness with the light growing ever dimmer. 'Stop!' he bellowed into his mouthpiece. The surface crew were concerned for his life, and asked him what the matter was. 'I am coming to an immense cavern. I cannot see the end of it, but the rope ladder is touching the floor of sand and pebbles and seems clear. Still 80 feet to go. Let go!'

Twenty three minutes after leaving the surface, Martel had reached the bottom of the shaft. Elated, but blue with cold and anxious about reports of storm clouds billowing high over Ingleborough, he quickly reconnoitred the cave, making the following notes:

'Gaping Gill is an abyss formed by erosion, a fissure enlarged by water, in the same way as the majority of the great caverns of the French Causses, but with this difference that a waterfall still falls into Gaping Gill. It is still being enlarged owing to the ceaseless fall of water. The vertical cascade of 325 feet, falling in a single column, and whose volume must be enormous after a storm or when snow is melting, proves that other abysses of this kind must be identical in origin, even when they are deeper and now completely dry . . . there is the feeble light of day which, filtering through the spray, with millions of prisms formed by the drops, does not seem like anything upon which the human eye has gazed. It affords one the impressive attraction of something never seen before. It is one of the most extraordinary spectacles it has ever been my pleasure to witness.'

Having completed his notes and made a sketch of the cavern, Martel prepared for the ascent, shouting his instructions into the waterlogged telephone. It did not work. He attached himself to the line and waited, bellowing out at the top of his voice, 'Pull! Pull!' He was yanked up, but after a haul of about 30 feet he was again left dangling.

He later recounts . . . 'I can hear nothing by telephone and the drenching waterfall continues inexorably to freeze me. At first I have a momentary distraction of seeing below me the remainder of my candle illuminations, whose light reveals the immensity of the cavern. But the stoppage becomes really past bearing. I try to climb up the ladder without the help of the lifeline but my limbs, stiff with the effects of the water, will not carry me more than a few rungs of the ladder.'

Exasperated at further delay, a dishevelled but ecstatic Martel was finally dragged to the surface after 28 minutes. And the sport of caving was born.

The
Wonder of
The Railway Age

One architectural feature above all others captures the spirit of the county: a monument in prancing stone, a symbol of bold endeavour and sacrifice raised to the hills, outstripping even the glories of York Minster as a totem to Yorkshire pluck.

The story of Ribblehead viaduct, more prosaically known as bridge No. 66 on the pioneering Settle to Carlisle railway, began with the vision and entrepreneurial spirit of the Midland Railway Company. Anxious to connect to the lucrative Scottish network, the company began work in the autumn of 1869. The theoretical task was simple, but the practicalities of driving a railway for 72 miles across some of the most inhospitable and wind-lashed terrain in Britain were difficult in the extreme.

The Tasmanian project engineer, John Sharland, who had the daunting task of selecting the optimum route for the new line, had an exacting brief. Notwithstanding the contorted geology of a landscape crowned with the forbidding summit of Aisgill at 1,169 feet, he was charged with designing a modern railway capable of carrying the fastest trains in all weathers.

The design was completed and the four tenders for individual sections of the route were let in the autumn of 1869. The successful tenderer for the length of line incorporating the viaduct was John Ashwell of Kentish Town, North London. The firm recruited a 60 strong team of masons and labourers and commissioned the building of a wheeled caravan, 'The Contractors Hotel' as a primitive site lodging for the geologists whose experimental borings would determine the positions of the piers. The caravan was towed from London by a steam engine and huts were erected alongside to house the labourers and their families. Few aliens to this wild place imagined the ordeals ahead.

All through the harsh winter of 1869-70 the men toiled, groping for bedrock through 25 ft of unstable ground. Pier support was provided by 6ft deep concrete piles and quarrying for the limestone superstructure was begun in nearby Littledale.

Over 30,000 cubic yards of limestone, in the form of giant 4 or 5 ton blocks were removed and on 12th October 1870 the imposing 24 arch span began to take shape, rising in a lattice of wooden scaffolding.

The logistics of the operation were impressive. In addition to the burgeoning shanty town of workmen's huts, it was necessary to provide a saw mill and a carpenters' shed, a blacksmiths' forge, stables, a pay office, a hospital, and a network of haul ways to facilitate transportation of materials over the sodden moor.

With the completion of the arches in 1875, the viaduct was virtually ready to be opened to traffic. Ballast and rails were laid and the directors of the Midland Railway Company, from the pampered warmth of a VIP railway carriage, viewed the product of their investment on 29th April 1875.

The price of this gargantuan achievement was heartache and pain, grinding labour, the disintegration of family life, lawlessness, drunkenness, injury, smallpox and sudden death. And all for wages of £1 per week.

The shock troops in this frontal assault on Yorkshire's wildest bastion were the labourers. They were accommodated mainly in huts, typically divided into three sections, for sleeping, cooking and dining. Despite the harshness of their surroundings, families managed to create some semblance of home, an 1870s visitor remarking 'The hardy wives of railway operatives decorated their wooden huts with paper hangings and pictures cut from illustrated newspapers and periodicals. They make substantial meals, keep good fires and study the comfort of their lodgers.'

A boon to the large colonies of rats was the plentiful supply of food. 'They had jovial doings among the hut inhabitants and were much given to nightly rompings above the ceilings.' The settlement was regularly visited by pedlars and it was reported that 'there is no lack of roast beef, savoury pastry, luscious fruits and beveridges of pleasant flavour to lovers of the bottle.'

Strong drink – succour of the oppressed worker – was both solace and scourge. Freely available from itinerant salesmen, from the 'Welcome Home', a licensed drinking den near the viaduct, and from two local public houses, liquor was responsible for a catalogue of foul deeds. Saturday night fist-fights were commonplace and there were incidents of wife beating, burglary and vandalism. On one occasion, a stupefied navvy tossed dynamite onto a blazing pub fire. Although the fireplace was blown out, he survived. The stupidity of a similarly afflicted worker was fatal. In a comatose state, he collapsed onto a haul way. The following morning an engine chugged along and chopped off his head! The 'Welcome Home' was a popular haunt of hardened drinkers. Two such reprobates stole money from the sleeping landlord to slake their thirsts. They were apprehended by the law and sentenced to three months' imprisonment with hard labour.

During construction of the railway, accidents and disease claimed the lives of some 200 souls. The cemetery adjacent to Chapel-le-Dale church had to be extended to accommodate the regular stream of interments. Worker fatalities resulting from accidents, failure of equipment and overwork were stoically accepted as the dire consequence of tackling one of the most challenging civil engineering projects in the world. However, death from diseases such as smallpox were particularly hard to bear as were fatalities involving women and children.

The daily grind was relieved by rare moments of comedy. A report of an amusing hospital incident was published in a local newspaper in 1874. The theme of the article was the workers' choice of beds – ditches, haul ways and coffins! The article was prompted by the experience of visitors to the morgue. They carried out an inspection of the receptacles for receiving victims of the plague and found one occupant there simply sleeping off the effects of strong drink!

The shanty town with all its passions and privations was but a transient star. Within a few short years of the railway opening, the wildernesss was returned to the sovereignty of the Three Peaks, the huts were dismantled and the graves were left to moulder. The Settle to Carlisle railway was opened to passenger traffic and exhilarating excursions by steam locomotive opened up a new chapter in railway history.

As interesting as the feat of construction itself is the story of the never-relenting need for maintenance, necessary to counteract the effects of thundering trains and foul weather. Shot-blast winds can scour the viaduct even in balmy May, sleepers can jump like staccato piano keys and hail and rain can pepper against the arches with a force which would shear sheep.

In 1947 and 1963 snow blocked the line for long spells and progressive deterioration of the viaduct went unchecked until major repairs were carried out during the 1970s. Faced with falling revenues and increasing maintenance liabilities in the 1980s British Rail, some might say rather cynically, reduced the frequency of trains in order to strengthen the argument for closure. The strong railway lobby was unimpressed and fought a sterling campaign to keep the line open. Thankfully, the government recognised the unique importance of the line and ordered a thorough overhaul of the viaduct. Traffic was stopped in October 1989 to allow repairs to be carried out. And here is a British Rail announcement...

'On Monday 30th October after two weeks of extensive renovation, the magnificent Ribblehead Viaduct will once again be open.

As well as the viaduct itself, we've carried out major work on three bridges along the route between Settle and Appleby, at a cost of over half a million pounds.

We believe it's money well spent, for the Settle – Carlisle line not only provides a vital link for many local people, but it passes through some of England's most spectacular countryside.

And as the line's future is now assured for many years to come, we hope you'll be among the thousands of people from all over the country who enjoy this wonderful journey.'

The Legend of Richmond Castle

Legend has it that a mystical sword lies underneath the romantic ramparts of Richmond castle, awaiting a knightly fist.

Many centuries past, in the balmy month of May, a band of gypsies came to the market town of Richmond, beguiling the country folk with charms and potions. A young maiden, Mary Thompson, her innocence lubricated by incautious amounts of gin, fell under their spell and dallied with one bespangled knave. In the moon-shadowed night, the youngsters caressed and fondled until at dawn's first peep the lad was gone, leaving only a golden cross and a chain slipped over Mary's neck with a parting kiss.

Mary never saw her lover again but when October came she had cause to remember his lusty ways. Richmond apples were not the only swelling fruits that autumn and Mary began to rue her night of glee. Attended only by an old washer woman, Mary was delivered of a son in the following spring and shortly afterwards she died.

Christened Peter, but known throughout the neighbourhood as Potter Thompson, the baby grew strong. A shy and introspective child, bullied by his elders and shunned for his quiet ways, he developed as a bluff and independent individual, taking up the stone-mason's trade.

Potter never married. A solitary walker and a regular

visitor to the banks of the Swale, he preferred his own company, and he would sit for hours musing over his tankard, fingering the golden cross given to him by his mother and wondering about the father he had never seen.

One day, as he took his usual stroll below the bastion walls, Potter halted and blinked, intrigued by a heap of newly fallen rock on the crag side. He scrambled up the slope to investigate, and found, behind the gnarled trunk of an ash tree, a narrow crevice. Thinking he had discovered an ideal shelter for inclement days, he squeezed inside, and found to his amazement that he was in a large cave. He stumbled forward with the breathless impetuosity of a child. Into the expanding void he shuffled, panting and perspiring and squinting at the blackness.

A veiled grey light, no more than a smudge, revealed the great size of the cave. Onward stepped Potter Thompson. And then he stopped, stock still, jack-in-the-box eyes spinning at an amazing sight.

In the centre of the cave was a magnificently carved and ornamented oaken table, and around its edge were 12 seated knights, time-frozen warriors, resplendent in armour and gaudy plumes. At their head was an even more imposing figure, a crowned king, his jewelled hands raised in prayer.

Hardly daring to breathe, Potter Thompson inspected the sleeping faces and he instinctively touched his golden cross. There was a sudden spark of life. The dust of centuries flew and Potter was gripped with mortal fear.

He must escape and tell his tale. But who would believe him? He needed evidence – a plume! a shield! What about that sword or horn on yonder table?

He picked up the sheathed weapon and, groaning at its weight, let it fall with a resounding crash. Reverberating through the cave, the echoes would have wakened the dead, but the noble congregation slumbered on. The diamond encrusted horn! Without thinking, Potter raised it to his mouth and pursed his lips, and was just about to blow when there was a creaking of long idle limbs and a communal yawn. 'Is it time?' rasped a stretching knight.

The startled Potter was off like a rabbit, running through the cave with a sepuchral voice ringing in his ears:

> 'Potter, Potter Thompson,
> If thou hadst either drawn
> The sword or blown the horn,
> Thou'd been the luckiest man
> That ever yet was born.'

Almost breaking his neck at the cave entrance, Potter raced home trembling and ashen faced.

During a sleepless night, he cursed his timidity and made up his mind to return to the cave at dawn. His heart racing, up the grassy track he came, intent on confrontation. But his way was barred. The entrance to the cave was sealed with unyielding rock. In wild frustration he clawed and pummelled the bloodied stone, finally flinging his golden cross petulantly into the river below.

And there it moulders. Perhaps if you were to scour the limpid pools you too could discover Excalibur!

The
Linton
Barghests

It is said that if you turn a Yorkshire sod, out pops a barghest or one of a score of other fanciful creatures. The folklore of our country is peppered with reports of vampires, ghouls, trolls, boggarts, bogies and wild men, but these apparitions can sometimes have a basis in fact as this illuminating tale from the village of Linton near Grassington shows.

Linton was once noted for flax, an attractive blue flowering plant also known as hemp, used in the manufacture of linen. Cultivated intensively by Giles Dakin, the squire of Linton Hall, flax was a lucrative cash crop whose sale amassed a fortune in gold, kept by its hoarder in a fortress-like bed.

Wealth begets avaricious whispers and news of Daykin's treasure came to the notice of three villains. Meeting in the parlour of the village inn, they plotted to steal the gold, arranging to enter Linton Hall through a side door leading from the flax sheds.

Supping rum, with only the comatose figure of landlord Boniface Platts for company, the men finalised their plan. At dusk they proposed to creep into the flax store and to tarry until midnight when the recumbent figure of Daykin and his gold would be easy prey. But publican Boniface, with eyelids clamped, overheard all the thieves' plans. As darkness fell, the men shook the seemingly sleeping Boniface, paid their dues and vanished into the night.

What was the eavesdropper to do? Undoubtedly he was a friend of the squire and yet he valued his life. Judging by their dress and demeanour, the burglars were from the tinker sect, a sometimes vile body of demons who would answer treachery with a vented throat. Old Boniface was scared. He looked for courage in the embers, found it in a glass of negus, wiped his chin and set off for Linton Hall. The publican and the squire almost collided in the gloom. Quivering, fearful of being overheard, Boniface whispered his warning and turned tail for the inn. Daykin, meanwhile, quietly entered his barn and overheard the mutterings of the tinkers. Now certain that he was about to be robbed, he left to rouse the town.

Waking neighbours from their slumbers he raised a sizable posse. Armed to the teeth and ominously bearing several ropes the vigilantes then surrounded the barn and dragged out the vagabonds and without more ado, the eldest of the group was hanged in Daykins's stable yard. Youth saved the other two cowering curs. They were sentenced to be stripped, ducked in the beck and tarred and feathered.

Water and tar proved no problem, but feathers were a different matter. Pluckings were in short supply, and to a comical roar, wool was used instead. Then the men were kicked into the darkness. In quivering terror, knowing that if they returned to Linton they would suffer the same fate as their comrade in crime, the men wandered the hills. Deranged by their experience they roared like wild beasts and stamped the ground, scattering the genuine sheep for miles around.

At daybreak a shepherd had the fright of his life. He stumbled across two hideous creatures. He described them thus: 'Like as you might say a couple of barghests, but stranger than usual – and I ran like hell!'

Croft Spa, Fount of Fantasy

The creator of probably the best loved children's novel in the world was born in the parsonage of Daresbury, Cheshire, in 1832. Here Charles Lutwidge Dodgson began the childhood imaginings which in later life became a hundred whimsical tales. But it was in a Yorkshire parsonage to which his family were despatched in 1843 that his literary genius blossomed, inspiring a story that has captured the hearts of children for generations. Today *Alice in Wonderland*, written under the pseudonym Lewis Carroll, is still a favourite on grandads' knees the world over.

Over the years the village of Croft Spa, a small riverside hamlet in North Yorkshire, has weathered the ravages of change, and Carroll's former home, the many windowed parsonage near the ancient church of St Peter's, remains. This perfect model for a dolls' house, a spacious and many roomed mansion set in a beautiful garden, was his delight and inspiration, and it was here, encouraged by a gaggle of younger sisters that he invented the games, shows and characters that were to be the substance of many of his literary fantasies.

A dark haired, shy, rather dreamy-eyed boy, with slight hearing and speech impediments, Carroll was always wary of adults, but even at 11 years old he displayed a natural talent for entertaining children.

With the help of a local carpenter he made a theatre with an attendant troupe of puppets, he constructed a toy train with its own station and booking office, and, exercising his already discernible flair for writing, he penned several family magazines and plays, including *The Tragedy of King John*, and the satirical *La Guida Di Bragia* – a ballad opera about Bradshaw's Railway Guide.

Other stimuli were the nearby woods and the banks of the romantic Tees. A compulsory, but invariably an inattentive visitor to St Peter's, he was further aroused by the sight of gargoyles, by the incredibly ostentatious pews of the local gentry, and by the often eccentrically clad parishioners, many of whom drowsed during the Reverend Dodgson's interminable sermons.

After only one year in Croft, Carroll was sent to the grammar school at Richmond where, despite the wrench from his family, he proved an able scholar. The rough and tumble of scholastic life toughened him physically, and he was remembered long after his departure as a boy who would fight for a good cause. Romantic Richmond with its fortress perched high above the river Swale further encouraged his creative mind and it was in Richmond that his first literary venture, *The Unknown* – a stirring mystery thriller for the school magazine – was published.

He left Richmond in 1846 for Rugby School and there he spent three tiresome and rather lonely years, relieved only by holiday visits to Croft. He read classics and mathematics, completing his studies with considerable success in 1849.

A gentle, and in many ways a naive student of 18, he returned again to Croft in 1850 to prepare for his entry into Oxford University. Although he studied hard, he still found time to resume the idyllic pastimes of his childhood, finding new excitement in Croft's expansion as a popular spa – a fast developing rival to Harrogate.

In this joyously happy year of 1850, he produced ambitious family magazines, notably the *Rectory Umbrella* a miscellany of parodies, stories and poems. The poem about his beloved parsonage was an especial favourite:

'Fair stands the ancient Rectory
The Rectory of Croft,
The sun shines bright upon it,
The breezes whisper soft.
From all the house and garden
Its inhabitants come forth,
And muster in the road without,
And pace in twos and threes about,
The children of the North.'

Reluctantly he left Croft in January 1851 to begin his studies at Oxford. Only 2 days later, however, he was recalled home for the funeral of his mother, of whom he wrote:

'Here may the silent tears I weep,
Lull the vexed spirit into rest,
As infants sob themselves to sleep,
Upon a mother's breast.'

Dispirited, he returned to Oxford, where he studied diligently, only journeying north again on vacation. For two months in the summer of 1854 he holidayed in Whitby, where some say his ideas for the *Walrus and the Carpenter* and *Alice in Wonderland* were first conceived. In any event, it is certain that he whiled away many a happy hour on the famous strand, weaving fabulous tales amidst a coterie of attentive listeners. By now, his view of the world was that of the perennial child. Immersed in their dreams and their pastimes, it is said that he reached the very zenith of his existence.

Enjoying the haven of Croft in the summer of the following year, he composed a new family magazine, *Misch Masch,* also inventing his celebrated poem *Jabberwocky* – the most original and outlandish poetical work in the English language.

The inspiration for this nonsense came from the legend

of the Sockburn Worm, a mythical, monstrous beast reputed to have been slain with a great sword near Croft in the years before the Norman Conquest. The instrument of the creature's demise was, until the early 19th century, presented to each newly elected Bishop of Durham as a token of his authority. In the later years, this ceremony took place on Croft Bridge, within yards of the Dodgsons' home.

Like his father, Carroll followed a religious vocation, and in 1861 he was ordained as a deacon by the Bishop of Oxford. For a time he delivered occasional sermons and he tutored small boys. Such, however, were the often cruel jibes about his twin afflictions, that he quit both pulpit and classroom, declaring afterwards that he would not teach young boys again even for £10,000 per year!

About this time he became sullen and unsociable with his adult colleagues, and yet, paradoxically, his inclination for the company of little girls, nurtured by countless hours of sisterly adulation, grew even stronger. To the embarrassment of some of his peers, he developed friendships with scores of devoted listeners, three of whom, in particular, were to change his life.

By 1862 he had shown considerable expertise in the new art of photography. Three of his more photogenic subjects, the charming small daughters of his mentor Dean Liddell, became his constant companions, especially during the warm summer months, when he would beguile them with picnics and episodes of a fantastic tale – the culmination of 25 years of make-believe. Captivated by images of a carved rabbit he had discovered in St Mary's Church in Beverley, he began reciting his story.

'Alice started to her feet, for it flashed across her mind that she had never before seen a rabbit with either a waistcoat-pocket or a watch to take out of it, and burning with curiosity, she ran across the field after it, and fortunately was just in time to see it pop down a large rabbit-hole under the hedge.

In another moment down went Alice after it, never once considering how in the world she would get out again.'

Cajoled by the girls into committing the episodes to paper, he submitted a manuscript to a publisher, who received it with enthusiasm. By the time of his death, 200,000 copies of *Alice in Wonderland* had been sold. Today sales have run into many millions, and the tale has been translated into more than 30 languages.

In June 1868, the Reverend Dodgson died and Carroll paid a last melancholy visit north to arrange for his sisters' removal. For 36 years, this happiest of homes had been a fountain of dreams, but in September he left it forever.

Today the spa of Croft is dry, the enchanted rectory garden is diminished, and the once busy railway station has gone. And yet a certain magic lingers on. Musing by the banks of Tees, or contemplating the opulent and extravagant interior of St Peter's, the observant visitor may yet see glimpses of a white rabbit on his way to a very important date. Despite the harsh realities of the 1990s, Croft Spa remains an enchanting place.

The
Resurrection
of John the Piper

John Bartendale was a travelling minstrel, a ragged out of tune piper who earned a meagre living entertaining crowds in the populous town of York in the reign of King Charles I. A dissolute fellow who supplemented his daily takings by a little pickpocketing, John was inclined to run foul of the law, and he paid for his misdemeanours with many a flogging. This did not improve his melodies and in 1634 he had to put his pipe aside for good.

Arraigned before York Assizes, John was accused of a felony. He was found guilty of the crime and condemned to death by hanging. The date of the execution was set for March 27th, outside the notorious Micklegate Bar.

Performed in open country with few spectators, the gruesome deed was done and the body of John Bartendale was cut down and buried nearby. That would have been the end of the matter and the piper would never have been heard of again but for the carelessness of the hangman and the undertaker. What should have been a corpse was actually still alive . . . but only just!

The near asphyxiated piper had been saved from eternity by an insecure knot, the shoddy workmanship being compounded by the perfunctory shovellings of a grave digger who had been anxious to go to lunch. John

lay unconscious in his pit for several hours. Somehow, the very earth which should have smothered out the last vestiges of life, warmed him back to life. Under the beneficial balm of an earth bath he moved, and the tremblings of the sod were noticed by a passer-by.

Stepping down from his horse, a distinguished gentleman, a member of the Vavasour family from Hazlewood near Tadcaster, went to investigate, and with the help of his servants, excitedly exhumed the body with his bare hands. The soil was brushed from the piper's face, rejuvenating brandy was administered, and he was asked to tell his tale. Before long, word of the miraculous resurrection had spread into the city and crowds who had hitherto shunned the cacophonous piper assembled to see the show. A cart was brought and the piper, wrapped in Mr Vavasour's cloak, was trundled to York Castle. Having only left its mouldy dungeons just a few hours before, the piper was heartily grieved.

The law had to take its scrupulous course and the piper was brought before the next assize court trembling at his fate. But the assembled judges were perplexed. Never in the annals of jurisprudence had a criminal who had endured the ultimate sentence returned to face the same charge. In a profession driven by test cases, there was no precedent. Could a man be sentenced to death twice for the same crime?

Persuaded by the intercession of Mr Vavasour, a good Catholic, and swayed by the clamourings of York's citizens, the piper was spared, the judge remarking that God speaks in mysterious ways and who was he to interfere with Divine Providence?

Amid a great tumult and a roar of approval from the throng, John Bartendale was released from custody. From that day on he mended his ways and took up the honest trade of a hostler. He continued playing the pipe, with some improvement. Near strangulation is said to have improved his technique!

Selected Bibliography

Inside the North York Moors Harry Mead 1978
Bridlington and the Yorkshire Coast Ward Lock Guide 1950
The War of the Roses Hubert Cole 1973
History of Sherburn and Cawood W Wheater 1882
Yorkshire Rivers – The Ure Tom Bradley 1891
The Great War at Sea 1914-1918 Richard Hough 1983
Yorkshire Oddities Incidents and Strange Events
    S Baring-Gould 1874
Shanty Life on the Settle and Carlisle Railway
    W R Mitchell 1988
The Story of Ribblehead Viaduct W R Mitchell 1990
From Edenvale to the Plains of York Edmund Bogg (undated)
Countrygoer in the Dales Jessica Lofthouse 1974
A History of Harrogate and Knaresborough The Harrogate
    WEA Local History Group 1970
Gaping Gill Howard M Beck 1984
Yorkshire Gordon Home 1908
Fair North Riding Alfred J Brown 1952
Storm Warrior Ray Shill and Ian Minter 1992
The Rowing Life-Boats of Whitby A F Humble 1974